Salieri

RIVAL OF MOZART

Antonio Salieri, ca. 1803-04; engraving by Johann Gottfried Scheffner; *Allgemeine musikalische Zeitung* 7 (1804), *frontispiece.*

ALEXANDER WHEELOCK THAYER

Salieri

RIVAL OF MOZART

edited by
THEODORE ALBRECHT

with a Foreword by
F. MURRAY ABRAHAM

The Philharmonia of Greater Kansas City
Kansas City, Missouri
1989

ISBN 0-932845-37-1

Produced through the generous assistance of Leo V. Sapper,
and in co-operation with the Department of Music,
Park College, Parkville, Missouri 64152

Printed in the United States of America
by The Lowell Press, Inc., Kansas City, Missouri

Contents

Illustrations

Foreword

THERE ARE VERY FEW incidents of pure joy I have experienced in my career, but each of them shares the same quality of discovery, of surprise.

It's hard to describe to a civilian one's work as an actor, but imagine, if you will, watching yourself in a home movie eating, drinking, showing off, when suddenly you see yourself do something completely uncharacteristic of your "self." You are intrigued by the action and run the video back to look at it again, and sure enough you are surprised again. And again. And yet again.

Mozart achieves this creative state almost at will. I must have heard the same passages of music twenty or thirty times during the filming of *Amadeus,* but they never paled. In fact, they grew even more satisfying with repetition, a phenomenon that astounds me every time I encounter great art.

Salieri must have responded as any artist would have—with amazement, humility, envy and finally with gratitude. For in the end, the source of creation is available to all of us, and those who are blessed with genius are only messengers bringing good news to an otherwise dark, at times unbearable, world.

F. MURRAY ABRAHAM
New York, New York

Preface

IN LATE 1863 AND through much of 1864, while putting the finishing touches on his *Chronologisches Verzeichniss der Werke Ludwig van Beethoven's* (1865) and the first volume of his definitive *Ludwig van Beethoven's Leben* (1866), Alexander Wheelock Thayer penned, for serialization in *Dwight's Journal of Music* (Boston), what remains today the most extensive biography of the composer Antonio Salieri in the English language. While working primarily in Berlin and Vienna, Thayer had been a regular contributor to *Dwight's Journal* for a decade when, in mid-1863, he began a series of studies called "Half a Dozen of Beethoven's Contemporaries." The first installment, treating Adalbert Gyrowetz, was serialized in eight issues, running from July 25 to October 31, 1863.

With his second "Contemporary," Beethoven's sometime teacher Antonio Salieri, famed today as the villainous presence in Peter Shaffer's play and motion picture *Amadeus,* Thayer became more ambitious, prefacing his remarks on the elder composer by a four-part history of "Opera in the Family Hapsburg," which ran in *Dwight's Journal* from December 26, 1863 to February 6, 1864 (Chapter 1 of the present volume). Publication of Salieri's biography itself began on February 20, and ran for some nineteen issues, concluding on November 26, 1864. It is quite possible that editor-publisher John Sullivan Dwight became vexed with Thayer's apparent prolixity on subjects Salierian: in the October 15 issue, Thayer wrote that he would hurry to a conclusion, "because I cannot suppose others to feel my interest in the history, and because there must somewhere be a limit to an article prepared for a journal." Likewise, as a coda to his final installment of November 26, Thayer listed several articles from the *Allgemeine musikalische Zeitung* as "worthy of being translated," "very interesting," and "well worth translation," although by this time Dwight had probably bidden him *satis est!* In any case, after the two biographies of Gyrowetz and Salieri, *Dwight's Journal* published no more in the series "Half a Dozen of Beethoven's Contemporaries."

From the outset Thayer demonstrates his desire to deal objectively with the controversial Antonio Salieri, whose renown, then as now, rested on his alleged envy and self-confessed poisoning of Wolfgang Amadeus Mozart. Thayer's historical sketch of the Hapsburg preferences for conventional and even conservative Italian opera indicates at once why Salieri became the mainstay at Joseph II's court, while Mozart was merely a visitor when the Emperor suddenly developed a transitory taste for something different—German opera, for instance, as so graphically portrayed in *Amadeus*. Thayer deals effectively with the legendary boycott of Mozart's *Marriage of Figaro* supposedly engineered by Salieri, and, while admitting that Salieri may have viewed Mozart's increasing popularity with some bitterness, gives no credence to Salieri's rumored murder of Mozart. Oddly enough, given its Beethovenian conception, Thayer's biography of Salieri pays little attention to Beethoven outside of his early homage and the remarks in the deaf composer's conversation books concerning Salieri's mental and physical decline.

For the Beethoven specialist, the portrait of Alexander Wheelock Thayer (1817-1897) which emerges from these pages will be just as interesting as that of Antonio Salieri. Readers of his authoritative *Life of Ludwig van Beethoven* have long since come to regard Thayer as a writer of dry, albeit informative, prose, and may find refreshing the vitality and wit (not to mention some embarrassing awkwardnesses) which abound here. He openly expresses his admiration for such pioneers of modern musicological research as Otto Jahn and Friedrich Chrysander, while decrying the romantic concoctions of Elise Polko and the lack of critical discrimination which he perceived in the writings of Adolf Bernhard Marx. While he adapted much of his biographical material from Ignaz von Mosel's *Über das Leben und die Werke des Anton Salieri* (1827), Thayer nonetheless verified details as closely as he could, given his other activities, and was not averse, in his Salieri text, to calling Mosel an "old fogy" or an "infinite ass." As a patriotic American living abroad much of his adult life, Thayer was a Republican adherent and an ardent pro-Unionist, railing (in his biography of Salieri!) against James Buchanan, Jefferson Davis and the Confederacy ("rebeldom"). No wonder Abraham Lincoln rewarded him with an appointment as United States Consul in Trieste early in 1865!

My editing of *Salieri: Rival of Mozart* (admittedly a supplied title) is functional rather than ideal, with footnotes kept to a minimum. I have sought, largely without using the most scholarly flags and fanfares, to standardize names and titles in conformity with modern musicological practice (as opposed to that used, say, by historians), to clarify dates and identities, to modernize Thayer's punctuation, and to update the most archaic elements of his vocabulary and syntax (if not incomprehensible, at least distracting to the modern casual reader) while retaining the flavor of his lively prose. As with the title of the book itself, I also supplied titles for the chapters after several readings of the manuscript seemed to indicate the most convenient, if uneven, divisions in Salieri's life, especially as it interacted with Mozart's.

In adding his own material to that derived from Mosel's *Leben,* Thayer usually employed an inconsistent system of parentheses and brackets, which I have for the most part left intact while adding my own bracketed comments and clarifications, sometimes appending my initials or Thayer's to avoid confusion of authorship in the most important items. Most often, however, my work can be distinguished in context from Thayer's easily enough. The scrupulous reader to whom greater editorial detail is important may wish to consult a copy of *Dwight's Journal* and satisfy his scholarly curiosity.

While editing, I had at hand a copy of Mosel's *Leben* to verify Thayer's source, not only for accuracy, but also to double-check his translations where his English wording seemed unduly awkward or otherwise inappropriate. I suspect that much of the garbled material in Thayer's articles, as they were serialized in 1863-64, was a result of Dwight's inability to read his handwriting, especially when it dealt with obscure titles or names. Occasionally, however, I felt justified in retranslating a brief passage from

Mosel for the sake of clarity in context.

Beyond this, I checked most factual details against the modern research of Rudolph Angermüller, cited in the bibliography, as well as standard monographic and reference works on Mozart, Gluck, Haydn and their contemporaries. Despite the presence of these fine tools, I became convinced that Mosel's *Leben* itself deserves a full translation into English, with exhaustive scholarly editing; because of his personal acquaintance with Salieri and his access to Salieri's papers after the old composer died, Mosel's biography possesses an immediacy, charm, and ring of primary authority which no modern study (not even the book you hold in your hand) can hope to attain.

The present edition of Thayer's *Salieri* was occasioned by a "Mozart and Salieri" seminar which I taught at Park College in Spring 1989, and for which it served as a text. I had first become aware of Thayer's virtually unknown biography of Salieri through a passing reference in Erich Prieger's obituary for the American author, translated by J.S. Shedlock in the *Monthly Musical Record* of September 1897 (see bibliography). Finding no other references to the Salieri biography in the Thayer literature, I was happy to locate specific references to most of the serialized installments in Michael Ochs's bibliographical study in the Forbes *Festschrift*. Characteristic of *Dwight's Journal* during this period, Thayer's articles were printed in infinitesimal print—one wonders how much of this material was ever read, much less comprehended, by Civil War-era Americans.

Many hands from Park College pitched in to make the logistics of editing considerably easier, among them Betty Vestal, who engineered interlibrary loans with virtuosity, and T.S. Pennington, who gave valuable advice on computer compatibility. I am especially grateful to Camille Lloyd for her interest, patience and good humor in transferring my enlarged and red-ink-drenched columns from *Dwight's Journal* onto word processor disk. Albert Dusing, of the Park College faculty, contributed fine photographic reproductions, to add interest to Thayer's previously unillustrated biography. Several students also lent their labors to this project, among them Vonceil Allen, Jeffrey Anderson, John Fowler, Heather Slocum and Donald Weiss. My gratitude to all!

At the conclusion of the seminar, I made the edited material available to the board of directors of the Philharmonia of Greater Kansas City (which, happily, I also conduct as part of my duties at Park College) to produce in book form as a benefit for the orchestra. William D. Hayes of the Philharmonia board provided his solid, practical marketing expertise, and Elaine Schwensen, the orchestra's administrator, spent long hours and days fine-tuning the manuscript, and making an abundance of frustrating logistical details seem easy. Irving Godt, Indiana University of Pennsylvania, kindly read through the manuscript, providing editorial advice and factual information on a host of subjects, from ancient Greek legend to the modern Italian language. Payson Lowell and Sharon VanHandel of The Lowell Press proved collaborators of the first order, generous with their advice, talents and expertise.

A distinctly separate word of gratitude must go to F. Murray Abraham, who kindly contributed the Foreword for this volume. His Academy Award-winning portrayal in the film *Amadeus* has created a public image of Salieri that (complicity in Mozart's death aside) remains a model of taste, accuracy, and dramatic art at its best.

With the deserved popular enthusiasm for Peter Shaffer's *Amadeus* in the 1980s, interest in the fictional and historical Antonio Salieri has never been greater, and with the approach of the bicentennial of Mozart's death in 1991, it is not likely to abate. My colleagues and I therefore hope that the reappearance of Thayer's *Salieri* after a century and a quarter of obscurity will lead to a further understanding of the relationships among Wolfgang Amadeus Mozart, Antonio Salieri and the Hapsburg Vienna in which they both moved.

THEODORE ALBRECHT
Park College

Antonio Salieri in middle age. This print may have been the source for the engraving in *AmZ,* 1804 (see *frontispiece,* above) Landon, *Haydn: Documentary Study,* pp. 158, 221, cites a copy in the Bertarelli collection [Biblioteca Trivulziana], Milan.

Antonio Salieri, February 6, 1821; lithograph by Friedrich Rehberg. Although made two decades apart, the portraits facing each other on these pages are remarkably consistent, and may represent the most accurate likenesses of the composer.

Alexander Wheelock Thayer in old age. Photograph by Sebastianutti & Benque, Trieste. Frimmel, *Beethoven Jahrbuch* 2 (1909). Thayer was only forty-six years old when he penned his biography of Salieri.

Introduction

BEFORE ATTACKING THE memory of Salieri, i.e. with biographic malice prepense—and in all friendliness to the little dark man, who really played a great part in his day and generation—I must put you through a short course of another diet and inflict *quant. suf.* of rather, but not too, dry matter upon your digestion. That is to say: for ulterior purposes, I wish the readers of *Dwight's Journal* [in which this material originally appeared] to be somewhat at home in the private musical life of the family, the heads of which have for so many centuries been rulers of such a large share of Eastern Europe, and more especially to be able to form some definite idea of the relations of the Hapsburgs to the old Italian opera. The question why Emperor Joseph II did not perceive at once the merits of Mozart and place him at the head of the Vienna opera instead of retaining Salieri as Kapellmeister and composer, will answer itself if these relations be once understood. Not that anything about to be written in the introductory sketch [Chapter 1] will have direct bearing upon that point—indeed the date of Mozart's advent in Vienna will not be reached—but the origin and strength of the taste of the Austrian imperial family for the Italian opera of the time will appear and be explained.

The basis of the background sketches of Chapter 1 is to be found in certain articles under the signature of "B---r" in the Vienna *Recensionen,* 1858, and part of the materials in Würzbach's *Biographisches Lexicon* of the Austrian Empire.[1] Since I know of no source in the English language where the informa-

---

[1] Constantin Würzbach, *Biographisches Lexicon des Kaiserthums Österreich,* 60 vols. (Vienna: W.K. Hof- und Staatsdruckerei, 1856-1891).—T.A.

tion proposed to be compendiously embodied here can be drawn, it is certainly to be hoped that it may prove of musical-historic value if not of interest—and, who knows, but some American Polko[2] may find inspiration in it for a dozen musical novels?

The basis of the biography itself is, of course, the short work (212 pages, 8vo) upon Salieri, by Mosel, a great portion of which consists of notices of the composer's works—a kind of writing which is seldom very satisfactory. In certain cases descriptions of forgotten compositions have an interest; for instance, Chrysander's analyses of Handel's operas are a valuable feature of his noble biography of that master, as they give us an idea of the causes which made him the most renowned musician of his day, long before the production of *Samson, Messiah,* and the other great works of his last period. They are also interesting in themselves as opening to us a way to gain some knowledge of the form, spirit, style, and effect, of what were held to be the grandest operas of that era. Salieri, however, lived too near our own time [1863-1864] to have any such interest connected with his works, that is in any high degree, and I shall spare the infliction of long disquisitions à la Mosel upon long forgotten works. The main thing, the principal object in view is, and will be, to enable the reader to live in Vienna, back in the days when Haydn, Mozart, and Beethoven were the greatest, but by no means the only great composers—and to become acquainted with a phase of Viennese musical life at that time, which their biographies except for a few years in Mozart's time, do not exhibit to us, but which nevertheless is necessary to anything like an adequate conception of that musical world, of which in one direction they formed by far the most important part. For personal interest, the narrative of Salieri's life is not to be compared with that of Gyrowetz;[3] and indeed, the principal inducement to write or read it lies in the fact that seventy-five years ago in all Europe, no operatic composer stood, on the whole, so prominent before the world as he, except Gluck, whose career was just closed, and

[2] A reference to Elise Polko, 1823-1899, German author of musical novels and collections of anecdotes.—T.A.

[3] The subject of a shorter biographical sketch by Thayer in *Dwight's Journal of Music* 23 (1863), Nos. 9 *et seq.* and Nos. 20 *et seq.*

Mozart whose great successes were so speedily to be followed by his death. I say upon the whole, for he had great contemporaries—what if their names are now seldom heard? Piccini, Grétry, Paisiello are certainly familiar enough, and a mass of German names might be added, which are associated intimately with the development of operatic art not in their own land alone, but south of the Alps. It is unfortunate for Salieri's fame out of Austria, or rather, I should say, in England and America, that his name is hardly known except in connection with his opposition to Mozart, which is so fully treated in Holmes's beautiful biography of the latter. For the present let that pass. His sins against Mozart have been punished sufficiently, whatever they were, and perhaps a cool judgment, if Salieri's side of the question could be presented with as much warmth as the other has been, might decide after all, that his fame has been clouded even beyond his deserts. I confess to a sort of liking for the little, dark, miserly, quaint, odd, rather vain (I judge), and envious Italian.

"For Heaven's sake, what *can* you find to like in such a character as that?" say you.

Perhaps because nobody, hardly, now-a-days, speaks of him except as the enemy of Mozart, nobody has ever thought it worthwhile (in English) to take him up because he is only a mark to cast stones at—like poor Süssmayr. You know what Touchstone says about Audrey: "A poor virgin, sir, an ill-favored thing, sir, but mine own; a poor humor of mine, sir, to take that no man else will."

But there is another reason for writing the history of Salieri, and no less a one than that he was the successor, so to speak (as will be seen), of him who wholly changed the character of the serious opera—not for one land alone but for the world—who, but Gluck?— and for years ruled that stage on which that change had been wrought. Among the strange absurdities which are current in the musical world are these two: the one, that what is now understood under the terms of grand symphony and string quartet—that is, the quartet and symphony written in C.P.E. Bach's sonata form, originated in Paris; the other, that it was there that Gluck developed and exemplified his operatic theory, and fought the great battle. Haydn and Mozart (to be followed by Beethoven) were the reformers and developers of instrumental music, and carried it to the highest point which it has yet reached—both laboring in Vienna; while Gluck and Mozart, at the same time, in the same city, and in the same way, were acting upon the character of opera.

Not until Gluck had founded a school was he engaged for Paris, and the contest there was in fact not so much between the two composers, Gluck and Piccini, as between the Italian and the Viennese schools—between the idea which Gluck had aroused in his mind by hearing (1745 and those years) works of Rameau in Paris, and of Handel and Dr. Arne in London, and which some dozen or fifteen years of reflection had ripened into materials for a system—and on the other hand, the ideas, which lay at the foundation of the old opera in general.

The biography of Salieri is for many years a history of that stage on which Gluck fought his battle, his success in which led to his engagement in Paris, where with the Austrian members of the French Court (Marie Antoinette and her party) upholding and aiding him, he carried the day on the boards of "La nouvelle Salle du Palais-Royal." Wonderful as the change wrought by Gluck appears, when his own works are compared with those of his old school contemporaries, it is far from being so striking as when we study this change by taking Mozart's operas for our comparison. As Haydn was the *inventor* in [classical] instrumental music, and Mozart the *perfecter*, so was Gluck the inventor and Mozart again the perfecter in the opera. A certain one-sidedness of Haydn is not reflected in Mozart, and the remark is equally true if we read of "Gluck" instead of "Haydn." Salieri possessed great native genius, and was an eclectic; hence in his hands the Viennese school, of Italian opera at least, profited by the labors of all his great contemporaries.

But one must be careful, when writing a preface beforehand, lest he say more than the subsequent work will justify; therefore let us stop here.

A. W. T

CHAPTER 1

Opera in the Family Hapsburg

As we have to do with Emperors and Empresses, with crown princes and princesses, archdukes and archduchesses, with a king or two now and then, we must find some means of fixing when they lived—we must have a date for a starting point.[1]

Anno 26 post urbem (Boston) *conditam, anno 26 ante urbem* (Philadelphia) *conditam, anno 30 post urbem* (New York) *conditam* (i.e. when the Dutch built the block-house on Manhattan Island), *anno*—say, *Anno Domini* 1656. It is the last year of William Bradford's Governorship of Plymouth Colony; the second year of John Endicott's third term as Governor of the Massachusett's [*sic*] Bay, the twentieth year of Harvard College, and the fifth of John Eliot's town of praying Indians at South Natick.[2] Roger Williams was elected last year President of Rhode Island and Providence Plantations; John Webster is serving his one year as head of the Colony on the Connecticut River. Peter Stuyvesant, last of the Dutch Dynasty, is in the tenth year of his rule over "die Nieuw Nederlandt," Communipaw and the countries beyond—now forming part of that region known variously as the "State of Damden and Amboy," "Copperheaddom" and New Jersey, and of that distant settlement of Swedes and Finns on the further side of the waters now called Delaware Bay; which settlement was conquered by the mighty Stuyvesant only the last year. Samuel Matthews was Governor of the Colonies in Virginia, and

---

[1] Blessed be the man that first invented dates! That discovered chronology to be the eye of history, as we used to study in Daniel Whelpley's *Compend* years ago, in J.Q. Adams' administration.—A.W.T. [Daniel Whelpley (1766-1817) was the author of *A Compend of History from the Earliest Times*, published variously in Philadelphia, New York, and Boston, but probably read by young Thayer in its 10th edition (Boston: Richardson and Lord, 1828).—T.A.]

[2] Thayer, of course, was born in South Natick, and graduated from Harvard.—T.A.

1

Catholic Maryland was in charge of Commissioners sent over by the Puritan Parliament. England had not yet generously begun to empty her prisons, jails and pauper-houses into the wilds of North America, and hence the country of the "Confederate States"—known briefly as "Rebeldom"—was still uncolonized. Beyond the ocean the grandest man who ever ruled the destinies of England—the Puritan farmer Cromwell—was drawing toward the close of his glorious career.[3] Baptist tinker Bunyan was ordained to teach and preach only last year by the congregation at Bedford; and the learned Mr. John Milton, the other great literary creative genius of that generation, now in his forty-eighth year, is Latin Secretary to Parliament, or his Highness the Lord Protector, I do not know which—perhaps both—is living, as nearly as I can make out, a second time a widower, blind, but in easy circumstances, down in old Scotland yard, convenient to Whitehall. The play house, so long suppressed by the Puritan and Presbyterian rule, shows signs of resurrection for Cromwell (1656) allows noseless Sir William D'Avenant to produce at Rutland house entertainment in "declamation and music, after the manner of the ancients," which he calls operas(!). Shakespeare has been quietly reposing just forty years in the church at Stratford; "rare Ben Johnson," nineteen years in Westminster Abbey; and John Dryden is a young man of twenty-five still at Cambridge, I suppose, who as yet seems to have done nothing in letters but compose a poor poem on the death of a certain Lord Hastings.

And so we get to the starting point.

The first two years of tinker Bunyan's preaching were the last two years of the reign of Ferdinand III, *Dei gratia,* King of Hungary, Bohemia, Rome, Archduke of who can tell how many states, and Emperor of Germany—an association of ideas which will enable ten to remember when the Emperor died by referring to the tinker, to the one who will fix the tinker in his mind by reference to the Emperor. There has been one Shakespeare, one Raphael, one Michael Angelo, one Handel, one Beethoven, one

---

[3] My admiration for that great and pure man dates long before Nutshell Carlyle had fallen down and worshipped him, i.e. publicly. [Thomas Carlyle, opinionated essayist and historian, 1795-1881.—T.A.] The utter worthlessness of the Nutshell-Epic poet's estimate of character is shown in his deification of that old brute, Friedrich Wilhelm I of Prussia. When he has finished whitewashing the Fredericks, let him try his hand at Pope Alexander VI, Jefferson Davis and James Buchanan.—A.W.T.

Bunyan—but as for Emperors!

In July 1656, Ferdinand III, Emperor of Germany, for the last time celebrated his birthday in one of the summer palaces near Vienna, for on the 2nd of April following he died. He was a practical and theoretical musician, and the last musical illustration, but one, in Athanasius Kircher's *Musurgia,* Vol. I, is an Italian vocal composition by him in four voices and a figured bass. An extract from a *Miserere* which he wrote is contributed by a correspondent to the Leipzig *Allgemeine Musikalische Zeitung* for 1826, cols. 503-504. An ancient publication at Prague was an aria with thirty-six variations, also from his pen.

At this last birthday festival was performed a "Drama per musica" entitled *Theti,* in five acts with ballets, text by Diamonte Gabrielli, music by [Antonio] Bertali, imperial Kapellmeister. At the close of the opera Ferdinand's son and successor, Leopold, already king of Hungary, as British heirs apparent to the crown are princes of Wales—"danced a ballet with eight sea-gods."

Ferdinand died on April 2, 1657, and the previous deaths of his three older sons now placed the hereditary crowns upon the head of the fourth, Leopold I, who was soon after elected also to the German imperial dignity.

Leopold had been intended for the church and his education, of course, had been in that direction during his childhood and gave him a fondness for science and letters which he cherished through life and for which he did much. He was but eighteen years of age when his father died and he found himself in a position to deny himself no desire of his heart. He inherited the Hapsburg passion for music and one of his first acts was the erection of an opera house hard by the palace, on the spot where now the imperial library contains the musical collection, which during the almost half century of his reign he brought together. In 1683, when the Turks besieged Vienna, it was found necessary to remove the theater because, being a wooden structure, the "Greek fire" of the enemy endangered the palace.

Leopold called Padre Kirchner (not Kircher of the *Musurgia*) from Rome to teach him counterpoint and under such excellent instruction the Emperor became a fine theoretic musician and a voluminous, if not great, composer; certainly there is no tradition that any of his works were damned. Imperial and royal works of literature and art are always successful at home. See the writings of Louis Napoleon Bonaparte for instance; or the church architecture of his late poor old Majesty, the last King of Prussia. In the Imperial Library at Vienna the musical productions of Leopold are preserved in quantities—oratorios, hymns, motets, music to operas, comedies and ballets.[4] He played the flute and had a spinet in each of his palaces at which he spent many of his leisure hours. He kept up an orchestra and complete troupe of singers both for the chapel and the theater. The vocalists and principal composers came, almost as a matter of course in those days, from Italy; that country which had for so many centuries been the center of the world's trade, art, religion, letters and vice and which, retaining the monopoly of artificial sopranos and altos [castrati]—who could have no other hope or ambition in life, than such as depended upon their perfection as singers—had carried vocal and, subsequently, instrumental music (until the enlargement and perfection of orchestras) to their highest pitch of excellence. When another nation shall become so rich and luxurious and its priesthood so debased as to fill its churches and theaters with that class of singers, then old Italy will be rivalled in the perfection of its vocal music.

Bertali was Kapellmeister at Leopold's accession, but after some half dozen years is heard of no more, "gone to his deathbed" probably [d. 1669], and Antonio Draghi's name occurs continually as composer of the court operas, in several cases both of text and music. "B---r"[5] says: "We will specially mention Antonio Draghi here on account of his almost unequalled fecundity, since in the repertoire of the Court Opera, which we have made running through a period of two centuries, this composer appears with 156 dramatic works which he composed for Vienna, and which were performed there." They begin in 1663 with *Oronisba,* to which Draghi also wrote the text, and end on November 8, 1699 with *Alceste,* text by Cupeda, ballet music by [Johann Joseph] Hoffer, which opera was performed on the birthday of Archduchess Maria, daughter of the King, afterwards Emperor Joseph I, by command of the Emperor. This composer had in

---

[4] For a list of the Emperor's works, see Rudolf Schnitzler, "Leopold I," in *New Grove.*— T.A.

[5] As noted in Thayer's Introduction, "B---r" is the otherwise unidentified author of pertinent articles in the Vienna *Recensionen,* 1858.—T.A.

Nicolo Minato, imperial court poet, an equally inexhaustible text writer. For, from *Atalante* (music by Draghi, ballet music by Schmelzer, performed on November 18, 1669 in honor of the dowager Empress Eleonora's birthday) to *Muzio Scevola* (music by Bononcini, imperial chamber composer, performed on the nameday of Empress Amelia), Minato wrote 110 textbooks [libretti] for Vienna.

The last text book "B - - - r" claims to have been *Muzio Scevola,* which was set to music by Handel, Bononcini and—who? Attilio, say all authorities except Chrysander, who gives Act I to Filippo Matteo, called Pippo, first violoncellist in the orchestra, and it is his business to know. Chrysander, too, says that the London *M. Scevola* text book was by Paolo Rolli, so here two doctors disagree.

Beside Bertali and Draghi, we have the names Cesti, Pederzuoli, Sances, Zaini as composers; Schmelzer and Hoffer composers for the ballet and two ballet masters. The "Chapel" [*Kapelle*], technically speaking, consisted of a chapelmaster [Kapellmeister], a vice Kapellmeister, three composers, five organists, thirty-four vocalists and forty-one instrumentists—a fine estalishment at a time when in Western Europe Louis XIV's "four and twenty fiddlers all on a row" were such a marvel.

The wardrobes and scenery of the court operas were very splendid and costly; for instance, the mounting of Cesti's *Il pomo d'oro* cost 100,000 florins—some $40,000—in those days when the comparative value of money was far greater than now [1863]. The regular annual expense of other court musicians was 46,780 florins, besides "remunerations." Leopold himself examined every candidate for his chapel, and every opera offered for performance; in the theater he always had the score of the music before him and it was no uncommon spectacle to see him directing the music of the mass from his box in the palace chapel.

His first wife cared nothing for music, but his second, Claudia Felicitas, from the Tyrol, played several instruments and sang well. She was shrewd too: at the Carneval of 1674, she caused to be performed an opera in three acts, entitled *La laterna di Diogene,* text by Minato, music by Draghi, in which various "court weaknesses" were brought to the Emperor's notice and even some lessons administered to him indirectly in the person of the

Alexander the Great on the stage.

Leopold showed the ruling passion strong in death. On May 5, 1705, he lay dying; he had received extreme unction and said his last prayer. Now he called for his orchestra and to the soft tones of their instruments breathed his last. Dramatic?

It must not be forgotten that the Italian language was as familiar at court as German, and that there were then no German opera and no German singers, at least in this part of the world. Even in North Germany it was only in a helpless infancy, not really flourishing even in Hamburg until the close of the seventeenth century. It is curious that English opera with Purcell and German opera with Keiser both flourished at the same time, and that neither then took firm root, both being crushed out by the Italian opera—but by an Italian opera composed by Germans: Handel, Hasse, and so on!

So Italian opera alone was known at the Court of Leopold, and in this and in the ballets the highest nobility and even members of the imperial family were often actors in the private performances of the palace. "B---r" furnishes a list which he was unable to make complete, since access to certain records was denied him, of such imperial and noble appearances upon the stage.

1661, May 9—*Il Ciro crescente, in tre Intermezzi, per Il Pastor Fido,* music by Bertali. This was given in the park at Laxenburg near Vienna on the birthday of Leopold, as introduction to a ballet in which Carl Joseph, the Emperor's brother, a boy of twelve years, danced.

A performance on January 24, 1667, affords a peep at the splendor of the young monarch's amusements. The occasion was his marriage (on the December 12th previous) with the unmusical daughter of Philip IV of Spain, his first wife. The piece was *La contesa dell' aria e dell' acqua, festa a cavallo,* text by Francesco Sbarra, with an equestrian ballet by Carducci, equerry called from Florence, the operatic music by Bertali, the ballet music by Schmelzer, the whole under direction of the imperial chief equerry, Count Dietrichstein.

Since there was no building in which this spectacle could be exhibited, an architect—Passetti—was called to Vienna from Italy and erected in the principal palace court a temporary structure, sixty feet high, supported on stone columns and arches, with three grand portals and spacious enough for the 5,000 spectators who "came from all lands" to witness the performances.

The marvellously poetic idea, which found local habitation in Signor Sbarra's production was this: the two elements Air and Water have a strife *(contesa)* as to which has the right to engender the pearl—Margareta, the royal bride—and call their brother (or sister, I do not know which) elements, Earth and Fire, to their aid. At first the quarrel is confined to words with musical accompaniment, but at last they seize their weapons and smite each other hip and thigh—as upon the rock Etam—until the Gods *and* the Emperor interfere and put an end to the contest. This ballet was produced by the nobility with fabulous magnificence. There are described in the text book—still preserved—twelve equestrian ballet figures which the Emperor led in person. Carl, Duke of Lorraine, was the Air; his ally, Fire, was acted by Count Raimund Montecucoli; Water appeared in the person of the Palatine Count Philip von Sulzbach, and Count Dietrichstein was Earth. The number of "acting and singing performers" was thirty-eight.

Margareta returned to the elements only six years after, dying on March 22, 1673; but Leopold comforted himself with the musical Claudia Felicitas on the following October 15th.

1667, June 9. *Vero amore fa soave ogni fatica,* text and music by Draghi, was an introduction "ad un nobilissimo ballo di 12 Dame etiope"; which is all the information I have upon this work.

1669, February 16. *Chi più sa manca l'intende,* opera in three acts with ballet, music by Draghi. The symphonies and ritornels were by Leopold, who also played the harpsichord part throughout the performance. The names Waldstein—of the famous Wallenstein race—and Mansfeld appear in the list of singers, that of Chilomonseck (queer Italian for Kielmansegg) as second violin. The two unmarried archduchesses, sisters of the Emperor, danced the ballet to Schmelzer's music.

Same year, November 18. *Atalante,* drama for music in three acts, text by Minato, music by Draghi, performed at the birthday festival of the Emperor's stepmother, Eleonore. At the close, ballet danced by her stepdaughters, archduchesses Maria and Eleonore.

1670, May 9. *Leonida in Tegea,* drama with ballet, text and music as above, with an aria in the third act by Leopold, on whose birthday festival the performance took place. Actors and singers were the higher nobility.

1670, November 18. *La casta Penelope,* musical drama in three acts with ballet; text and music, Minato, and Draghi and Schmelzer; on the birthday of the dowager Empress. The archduchess Eleonore was now deceased, but Maria as Virtue and four ladies of honor as assistant Virtues danced the ballet in the temple of Virtue.

1671, June. The young Counts Königseck and Wallenstein danced a Sarabande, music by Schmelzer, in honor of the Emperor's birthday.

1671, November 9 [18?]. *Cidippe;* musical drama, three acts, and ballet, by Minato and Draghi, with arias by Leopold; on the Empress mother's birthday. At the close, archduchess Maria and four ladies of honor represented Diana and nymphs.

1672, February 21. *Sulpitia;* musical drama and ballet by Minato, Draghi and Schmelzer, on the name-day of the dowager. Archduchess Maria and ladies of the Court represented this time Glory and the heroic virtues.

1672, February 2.[6] *La Tessalonica;* musical drama, three acts, and ballet, by Minato, Draghi and Schmelzer, on the dowager's birthday; at the close archduchess Maria, Marchesa Trivulzia and four young Countesses performed a "Dance of Happiness."

1673, Carneval. *Artemisia.* Three acts, and three ballets, text by Minato, music by Draghi or Cavalli, performed by the ladies of the court on the private stage as fast-night amusement.

1674, November 10. *La nascità di Minerva,* festive piece with ballet, by Minato and Draghi, on the dowager's birthday, on the private stage. Archduchess Maria and five ladies danced a representation of "Cheerfulness."

1676, June 9. *Il Seleuco,* musical drama [by Draghi], with ballet, on the Emperor's birthday. The ballet was "The dance of the Morning Star, ten early stars outshining," by the archduchess Maria Antonia and ten ladies of the court.

---

[6] Efforts to correct and amplify Thayer in this introductory chronology must necessarily remain limited, but details may be compared with work lists in "Antonio Draghi" and other pertinent articles in *New Grove.*—T.A.

1676, November 22. *Lo specchio,* a cantata for five voices by Minato and Draghi, sung by "an Archduchess" and four Countesses.

1677, November 18. *Rodogone,* musical drama, three acts, with ballet by Minato and Draghi, performed in the private theater by the nobility on the Empress mother's birthday. The archduchess Maria Anna with five ladies danced a representation of "Shrewdness" (*Klugheit*).

1680, November 15. The Court was in Linz. In honor of the name-day of the Emperor, the archduchess Maria Josepha and six ladies of the court danced a ballet, music by Schmelzer.

1682, November 24. Prince Ludwig of Baden and gentlemen of the Court performed a ballet, *Gli Fentoni,* music by Schmelzer.

1682, Carneval. An introduction, vocal piece, text by Minato, and a gypsy ballet, music by Pederzuoli, performed by the King of Poland, the Duke of Lorraine, and the Empress mother's ladies.

1682, June 9. *Il sogno delle Grazie,* introduction to a ballet by Minato and Draghi. On the birthday of the Emperor at Laxenburg, performed by archduke Joseph, archduchess Maria Antonia and ladies of the court.

1684, Carneval. *Il finto astrologo,* with a comedy and ballet, by Minato and Draghi, performed by the nobility.

1685. "The Recreations of the Female Slaves in Samia," an interlude with German and Italian text by turns, music by Emperor Leopold, and performed by the Empress mother's ladies.

1685, Carneval. "Scherzo musicale," in the "manner of a scenic representation;" Minato and Pederzuoli, "Kapellmeister of the Empress," performed by the ladies of the Empress.

1685, Carneval. *Amfitrione,* prologue by Minato and Draghi, performed by the Emperor's chamberlains.

1686, Carneval. Three pieces are given in "B---r's" list. "Musica per una festa," by Minato and Pederzuoli, performed by archduchess Maria Anna, the Elector Palatine, with ladies and gentlemen of the Court.

[1686.] Music to a "Comedia" of the "noble ladies of the court," with alternate German and Italian text by the Emperor Leopold.

[1686, October 12?]. *Il ritorno di Teseo dal labirinto di Creta,* introduction to a ballet, by Minato and Draghi; performed by the Elector of Bavaria and ladies of the Court, after Leopold's return from a campaign.

1688, November 15. *Il silenzio d' Harpocrate,* musical drama, three acts, text and music by Draghi, on the Emperor's name-day, performed by the nobility.

Thus, we have reached the date of the English Revolution and the final expulsion of the Stuarts; and nothing is more natural than to compare the elegant and chaste amusements of the imperial family at Vienna with those of the royal family of England, during the period we have had in review. The former are purely aesthetic—poetry, music, and the dance combine to do honor to the mother or brother, the Empress or Emperor, in illustrating virtue or representing pure subjects from ancient mythology—the fashion of that age. But he who has had occasion to study the dramatic literature fostered by Charles II or his brother and successor James, knows what a perfect moral *cloaca* the English stage was; and not only what filth was uttered in public by actresses, but what filth was written by women themselves for public utterance. I challenge the production of a loose expression in all these works still preserved in the imperial dramatic archives in Vienna. That in the popular German drama of that age there is much which could not now be revived is certain; but it is chaste in comparison with the contemporaneous English drama, and its humor of that kind does not measure its success by the degree of its filth and obscenity.

1689, Carneval. A ballet, music by Schmelzer, danced by the Queen of Poland and other ladies of the Court. Arias by the Duke of Lorraine.

1689, November 15. *L'Harpocrate* again, performed by the nobility on the Emperor's name-day. Probably the text was re-written, since Minato's name appears.

1690, June 9. *Scipio conservatore di Roma,* musical drama [by Draghi], one act; performed on the Emperor's birthday, by the nobility.

1692, Carneval. *La chimera,* fantastic drama, three acts, by Minato and Draghi, performed by the nobility. In this piece were ten "singing persons," among whom were:

Cottis, a lunatic of various fantasies—Count Zernini.

Acce, a female zany of various follies—Franz Zernini.

Hipparcho, an astrologer—Count Waldstein.

Arpesia, in love, but not believing anything her lover says—Fräulein Countess Waldstein, etc.

The first ballet was of fishermen, danced by six nobles; the second of herb-women, by seven countesses; the third of negroes, by four nobles, and as many women of high rank.

1690. (1693?) "The First Fruits of Virtue Exhibited in Young Cato of Utica." This was a drama in German, but with music and dances. Of the twelve performers, six were children of the Emperor:

Cato—Joseph, aged 15.

Cepio—Carl, in his 7th year.

Portia—Elisabeth, in her 13th year.

Livia—Marianna, in her 10th year.

Julia—Therese, in her 9th year.

Cornelia—Josefa, 6 years old.

1695. Festival music composed by the Emperor and performed by the archduchesses.

1697, Carneval. *Musica per la Comedia,* German, Italian and French text alternately, music by the Emperor; performers the archduchesses and ladies.

1697, November. *Sulpitia* again, but with alterations and arias by the Emperor, new ballets with music by Hoffer, on occasion of Leopold's name-day.

1697, Carneval. Musical interlude, by Minato and Draghi, *Se sia più giovevole la fortuna o il merito?*, sung by four ladies: "Confidenza, Speranza, Prudenza, Avertenza."

1698. *L'Amazona Corsara,* musical drama, three acts; music by Badia, performed by the nobility.

1699, February 28. *Imeneo trionfante,* Serenata, music by Badia. This "Triumph of Hymen" was produced upon occasion of the marriage of archduke Joseph, in the large court of the imperial palace. Thirteen large open coaches formed a procession which, entering the court, drove round and came to a stand in a circle, when the Serenata was performed. Three of these vehicles were very magnificent; the central one conveyed Hymen, Jupiter, Hercules, Juno, Hope, a Good Genius, Youth, Pleasure, Union, and a number of Athenian virgins, who were set at liberty by Hymen.[7] In the carriage on the right were Apollo, the Seventeenth Century (!), Time, Joy, Leda, Diana, and the four Continents surrounded by the most celebrated poets [representatives] crowned with garlands. On the left rode Venus and the Graces, Cupid, Mars, Bacchus and Mercury with Tritons and Nereids. The other ten carriages were full of gods and goddesses (the singers and orchestra).

Here I would suggest that the term "Serenata," as applied to such works as Handel's *Acis and Galatea,* may well have had its origin in performances of this kind; for the "Serenata" may be called a short opera, to be performed in costume but without action, precisely the kind of performance which suited a stage consisting of coaches, in an open court for the theater. Nor was the Serenta, thus understood, any novelty in Vienna. "B - - - r "cites a work dating from 1641 to the following effect:

> Next day there was a magnificent procession; for first came six triumphal cars in the palace court, drawn by small, white ponies, also by bucks and unicorns; on each splendid music, and thereby also trumpets, drums and other instruments were played. Then came Neptune with twelve whales in which many rustic pipes (*?Schalmeien*) were heard. Farther there appeared a garden with flowers and fountains, with Venus, and four mountains, with noble music and in splendid array. The last mountain and procession came to a stop before the windows of her Majesty, and a comedy was performed.

1699, November 15. *Il Sole; La Fenice, Il Tempo, Musica di Camera.* Text by Cupeda, music by Badia; performed on their father's name-day by "Joseph and his brethren," the archdukes and archduchesses, and gentlemen and ladies of the Court.

1700, February 28. A Prologue to the opera *Il Demetrio,* performed by Joseph and his wife, and his sisters, the archduchesses.

It would seem that Leopold's daughters were singers, not dancers like his sisters.

1700. *Diana rappacificata con Venere e con Amore,* musical drama, music by Badia, on the birthday of Joseph's Queen, performed by the nobles with some of the actors of the court theater.

---

[7] Why? Because, Joseph having taken a wife, they were free to seek husbands?—A.W.T.

This closes "B---r's" list of these private and family performances during the life of Leopold I.

Joseph I, Leopold's successor, had a short reign of six years but
a busy one, for it was the time of Prince Eugen of Savoy, and
John Churchill, Duke of Marlborough. Concerning musical and
dramatic doings at court (the reader may be glad to know) I find
no record. Joseph's only son died in infancy, and thus his brother Carl became his successor.

The young king, born in 1685 (October 1) only a few months
after Handel and Bach, was in Spain carrying on the war with
Philip V for the throne of that country when the news of his
brother's death (April 17, 1711) reached him. He hastened to
Vienna, assumed the various crowns which were hereditary in
the family of the Hapsburgs to which he added, by election, that
of the German Empire in October, and that of the Kingdom of
Hungary in the next May.

1711. Not an uninteresting point of time for us, though not
particularly so in our own land. There have been great political
changes in the colonies, most of which have now royal Governors
and many have been consolidated—for instance, his Excellency,
Joseph Dudley, appointed Governor by King William in 1702,
rules from Boston (the capital), Maine, New Hampshire, Massachusetts Bay, and Plymouth colonies, and a part of Vermont, if
there is anything up in the Green Mountains to be governed.
The Governor of New York, General Hunter, has jurisdiction also
over both East and West Jersey, and Charles Gookin, Deputy of
the English proprietors, rules both Pennsylvania and Delaware.
In New England, two little boys, who are to have no small share
in putting an end to this appointing of Governors in these
Colonies, are just learning to read; one of them, five years old, is
the son of Mr. Franklin, soapboiler in Milkstreet, Boston; the
other, Stephen, son of a Mr. Hopkins, in Providence, R.I., if my
memory does not deceive me.

But if we look "home"—as our forefathers in those days called
England—we shall see much to interest us, just at this date. The
Rev. Jonathan Swift, editor of that political sheet the *Examiner,* is
just giving to the public his "Proposal for correcting and improv-
ing the English Language," stolen bodily almost from Defoe's
"Essay on Projects," a man whom the Reverend gentleman hates

but plunders; young Mr. Pope is just bringing out his "Essay on Criticism;" and (my favorite Essayist) Steele has closed his *Tatler* and, with Addison—who has come back from Ireland—is producing the daily numbers of the *Spectator.* Defoe, a greater man than either, "unabashed Defoe," ready to sacrifice everything, life itself if need be, for the right, the strongest, noblest specimen of moral power of that day—without the qualities or desires which could enable him to be counted among the "wits" of Queen Anne's reign or to flourish at the coffee houses—is enjoying once more a gleam of sunshine, for the Sacheverell trial last season has made Harley minister again, and Harley has taken the Editor of the *Review*—the fearless, not earless, as Pope unjustly called him—to kiss her Majesty's hand. And Defoe, with a strength of conviction and power of common sense amounting to genius, is battling for the principles of the Revolution. Eight years are still to pass before, giving up politics, he is to produce the most original, delightful, popular and immortal work—*Robinson Crusoe*—which the world has seen since Bunyan's *Pilgrim's Progress.*

Handel's first opera written for England, *Rinaldo,* is having its wonderful success, and Addison, whose *Rosamund* has not proved a successful match against the Italian opera, is, in the *Spectator* ridiculing Rossi for calling (in the Preface to *Rinaldo*) "Mynheer Hendel the Orpheus of his age," and is making merry over the flight of sparrows introduced into Armida's garden in the same opera.

Carl VI, born October 1, 1685—had just completed his 26th year when crowned Emperor (October 12). He had all his father's passion for music, though not his fecundity in composition. I find no records of operatic music written by him, but he appears to have produced a pretty large quantity for the harpsichord and of vocal pieces in other forms, especially canons. A *Miserere* for four voices with figured bass, composed near the close of his life, is among his autographs. Like his father, he assembled distinguished musicians at his Court, examined the candidates for the office of Kapellmeister and the scores of operas presented for performance; and sometimes at private productions in the summer theater of the Favorita Palace, in the Augarten, he played the harpsichord from the full score. His master in counterpoint was the famed Johann Joseph Fux, whose *Gradus ad Parnassum* he caused to be printed in a splendid folio volume, dated 1725.

In free composition he was pupil of Caldara, who from 1716 to 1736, twenty years, produced fifty-two operas for the Court theater.

Carl's ear for music was celebrated; no fault escaped him, but a composition which satisfied him could arouse him to enthusiasm. "B---r's" reading of the old anecdote of the Emperor and Fux seems the most probable; namely, at the third performance of the opera *Elisa* (text by Pariati, music by Fux)—first given in the Favorita theater, August 28, 1719, on the birthday festival of Empress Elisabeth, Carl was so delighted with the music as to seat himself at the harpsichord and accompany the entire performance. Fux, deprived of his proper office, stood by and turned over the leaves, and at the close exclaimed, "Bravissimo! Your Majesty might very well take my office." "I thank you, my dear Kapellmeister, for your good opinion," answered the Emperor, "but I am very well satisfied with my own."

It is well known, continues "B---r," what a good influence Carl's advice exerted upon Farinelli—the *castrato*, of whom the Englishwoman said, "One God, one Farinelli." That famous singer was three times in Vienna, in 1724 (with Porpora), in 1728 and 1731. On one occasion, when the Emperor was accompanying him, he remarked how much his vocalism would gain if he would less frequently overload his melodies with such long-breathed ornaments. This advice was followed by Farinelli, and from this time dated the marvellous depth of expression of his adagios.

During Carl's reign there were four regular family festivals: the Emperor's birthday, October 1; his name day, November 4; the Empress' birthday, August 28, and her name day, November 19.

For November 4, the Empress provided an opera in the great theater, and for August 28, the Emperor one for the summer theater in the Favorita. These were but occasional works and, though produced with great splendor, were performed but two or three times each. The mounting of one of these operas cost from $25,000 to $30,000 [in 1863 dollars]. The costumes were of velvet and silk richly embroidered with gold and silver, the very members of the orchestra appeared in splendid dresses, and neither the opera in Paris nor in London could at that time, in the matter of the vocal and instrumental music, the costumes and decorations, stand any comparison with the imperial court theater of Vienna.[8]

The annual expense of Carl's opera was in round number $100,000 [in 1863 dollars]—of which 43,000 florins was for the "Chapel" [*Kapelle*] or musical establishment which was thus made up:

1   Court Kapellmeister, Johann Joseph Fux.

1   Vice Kapellmeister, Antonio Caldara.

3   Composers, [Carlo Agostino] Badia, Francesco Conti and Porsile.

2   Composers for ballet, Matheis and Holzbauer.

3   Italian court poets, Stampiglia, Zeno and Pariati, afterwards Pasquini and Metastasio.

1   German court poet, Prokoff.

34   men singers.

8   women singers.

1   concertmaster and his assistant.

32   players of string instruments, 2 theorbos, 1 viol di gamba, 1 lute, 5 oboes, 5 bassoons, 4 trombones, 1 horn, 13 trumpets, 1 drum.

There were also two ballet masters.

Prince Pio was general operatic director and the whole was under the charge of the *Obersthofmeisteramte* [*sic*]—which four words in one I take to be the equivalent of Lordhighchamberlain'soffice, the longer word by six letters. In the "Court-kitchen-department" was a special "musicians' butler" with two assistants. Of all retainers of the court, the musicians alone, when enfeebled and superannuated, still retained their offices and drew a salary.

Carl VI's regard for Fux is well known to all who are familiar with musical history. "B---r" gives a pleasant proof of it. In 1723, in August, the court was in Prague, and the celebration of the Empress' birthday (on the 28th) took place in a temporary the-

---

[8] I am not ready to admit this statement in one particular—namely as to the vocal music of the London opera, say from 1720 to 1735, for Handel was the composer of a very large proportion of the operas given, and the greatest vocalists then living were at various times engaged. In other respects, yes.—A.W.T.

ater put up for the occasion, a sort of amphitheater without roof. The opera was *Costanza e fortezza,* a festive piece by Pariati, with opera music by Fux, and ballet music by Matheis, written for a chorus of 200 voices and an orchestra of 100. As the day drew near, Fux was taken ill and had to make the journey to Prague in a litter. At the performance, the Emperor caused Fux to sit next to him in an easy chair as a spectator, while Caldara had the direction. But let Gerber tell these stories of Fux in his way:

Fux (Johann Joseph), imperial chief Kapellmeister in Vienna, born in Styria about 1660, filled this distinguished and honorable post some forty years, under the Emperors Leopold, Joseph, and Carl VI, all of them as thoroughly taught in music as a prince ever can be. The regard of this last-named Emperor for his old Kapellmeister went so far that, in 1723, being afflicted with gout, Carl had him transported from Vienna to Prague in a litter, where the old man had the pleasure to hear, sitting near the Emperor, his opera performed by 100 singers and 200 instrumentists. He took another method of showing his appreciation of Fux's talent the next year: on the occasion of the birth of an archduchess [Maria Amelia, April 5, 1724], Fux produced an opera which pleased the Emperor so highly that, upon the third performance, he made a lottery for the benefit of all who sang or played in it, with jewels, gold watches, snuff-boxes, etc., for prizes. All the tickets drew prizes, the least of which was of 500 florins value, the highest going up to 1000, 1500 and even 2000 florins. The eldest archduchess [the afterwards famous Empress Maria Theresa, then about seven years old, born May 15, 1717] sang in the piece on the stage, and the Emperor himself directed the entire performance at the harpsichord. As he entered the orchestra, the score of the opera, most splendidly bound, was presented to him in the name of the Empress, upon which the Emperor, after bowing to her, placed himself at the instrument and gave the signal to begin. It was on this occasion that Fux, who stood behind the Emperor, after noting many proofs of Carl's skill in the most difficult

passages and many a bravo! at last exclaimed, "Oh, it is
a pity that your Majesty has not become a virtuoso."
Whereupon the Emperor turned to him with the
remark, "No matter, I have it better as it is." [*Neues Lexicon,* article "Fux"]

Note how differently, both as to date and in form, this last
anecdote is given by my "B---r" and Gerber. Würzbach tells it
still in another form, and makes Leopold the hero of it instead
of his grandson. True, it is not very important just what words
were used on so trivial an occasion, but when you have had occasion to make yourself pretty familiar with almost all the works
produced in more than a century and a half in a certain department of literary and artistic history and find that a general and
all-pervading characteristic is an utter carelessness in repeating
facts and anecdotes, you begin to despair of ever getting at truth.
This is true to an astonishing degree of the Germans. They plun-
der one another for anecdotes and stories, yet rarely repeat one
without contriving to make it sound more or less differently. It
has only been about twenty-five years since Wegeler and Ries's
Notizen about Beethoven appeared; and yet their anecdotes have
little by little become so changed as often to be hardly recogniz-
able. So, A.B. Marx, in telling of Beethoven's trouble in the first
performance of his Choral Fantasia, though he had (or might
have had) the anecdotes as told by three persons present, follows
neither; but of all writers he is one of the very worst in this
respect—you cannot trust him a moment. Thank fortune, there
are a few conscientious writers even on music and in Germany
—Jahn and Chrysander for instance. Being easier after this
expectoration, I go back to Carl VI.

As on the nameday of the Emperor and the birthday of the
Empress new operas were given, so on the birthday (October 1)
of the Emperor, and nameday of the Empress (November 19),
there were given in the Palace at Vienna, "Serenatas."

And now again to "B---r's" list of the private "family" performances.

1722, January 17 and 24. *Aloïda,* comedy and ballet, performed by the nobility at court.

1724, May 16 and 18. *Eurysteo,* musical drama in three acts. Text
by Zeno, music by Caldara, with three ballets, music by Matheis.

Is it asked, how came Vienna—instead of London, which latter city had the greatest dramatic composer of his age, thirty-five years long giving her new works on an average one a year—to be during all the second half of the last century at the head of the world's music. Let an answer be found in the list of performers in *Eurysteo,* as given in the imperial palace.

Actors and Actresses in the Drama

Ismene . . . . the Italian Countess Orsini
Erginda . . . . .Judith, Countess of Staremberg
Aglatida. . . . . .Josepha, Countess of Berg
Ormonte . . . . C. Josepha, Countess of Gallerati
Cisceo. . . . . Carl, Prince of Savoy
Elearco . . . . Ferdinand, Count Harrach
Glaucia. . . . . Peter, Marquis Stelia

First Ballet

Rosalia, danced by . . . . Countess Thurn
Christine . . . . Countess Salm
Josepha . . . . Countess Henkl
Antonia . . . . Countess Sinzendorf
Carl . . . . Count Salm
Anton. . . . . Count Strasoldo
Joseph. . . . . Count Zobor
Christian . . . . Count Westenrod

Second Ballet

Ledly . . . . the Archduchess Maria Theresa (b. 1717)
Eleonora . . . . Countess Goes
Josepha . . . . Countess Fünfkirchen
Isabella. . . . . Countess Styrum
Francisca. Countess Thürheim
Friedrich. . . . . Count Schlick
Franz. . . . . Count Schrottenbach
Wenzel . . . . Count Bernier
Caesar . . . . .Count Capitani

Third Ballet

Maria Theresia . . . . Archduchess Maria Anna (b. 1718)
Amalia. . . . . Countess Althan
Anna . . . . Countess Serbelloni
Wilhelmine . . . . Countess Souche
Sophie. . . . . Countess Wrbna

Carl . . . . Count Althan
Leopold . . . . Count Kinsky
Peter . . . . Count Rofrano
Carl . . . . Count Cobenzl
Sigmund. Count Kehrenhüller

Orchestra

Harpsichord . . . . Ferdinand, Count Pergen
Flute. . . . . Ludwig, Count Salaburg
Bassoon . . . . Ferdinand, Count Cavriani
Bassoon . . . . Constantine, Baron Digher
Contrabass. Adam, Count Losy
Violin . . . . Christian, Prince Lobkowitz
Violin . . . . Ferdinand, Count Lamberg
Violin . . . . Christian, Count Proskau
Violin . . . . Carl, Count Apremont
Violin . . . . Joseph, Count Stubenberg
Violin. . . . . Carl, Count Natal
Violin . . . . Christopher, Count Pertusati
Violin. . . . . Casimir, Count Werdenberg
Violin . . . . Octavius, Count Piccolomini
Violin . . . . Franz, Count Pachta
Violin. . . . . Michael, Count Casari
Theorbo . . . . Adam, Count Questenberg
Oboe . . . . Count Truchsess von Zeil
Oboe. . . . . Siegfried, Count Lengheim
Violoncello . . . . Johann C., Count Hardegg
Violoncello . . . . Sigmund, Count Herberstein
Violoncello. . . . . Johann B., Count Pergen

Thus, every performer, whether singer, dancer or player of an instrument, belonged to the highest nobility of the Emperor's dominions. With such a nobility and with such an imperial family, is it strange that music should flourish? Especially in an age when there was no *public* for the higher music, as we understand the term, but when that kind of enjoyment was a luxury of the high born and wealthy, and when composers depended upon Maecenases for encouragement?

1729, March 2. *Sesostri,* tragi-comedy in three acts. Music by Porsile, performed at court by the nobility.

1735, Carneval. *I Cinesi,* a prologue to a ballet; text by Metastasio; music by Reutter; performed by the archduchesses Maria Theresa and Maria Anna, and ladies of the court.

During the same Carneval, another "Introduzione d'un ballo," text by Metastasio, music by Caldara, was given by the two young archduchesses and the Countess Fuchs.

Same year, August 28. *Le Grazie vendicate,* Serenata, text and music as above, performed privately in the Favorita palace by the two archduchesses, Prince Charles of Lorraine and a lady and gentleman of the court.

October 1. *Il Palladio conservato,* in one act—Metastasio and Reutter—on the Emperor's birthday, also in the Favorita, by his two daughters and Countess Fuchs.

1740, October 1. *Il natale di Giove,* in one act, text by Pasquini; music, Bonno; performed in the same place, on the Emperor's birthday, by his two daughters, Prince Charles of Lorraine, and a lady and gentleman of the court.

1740. *Attilio Regolo,* text by Metastasio, was written for the Emperor's name-day, November 4, but was not performed, owing to his decease on the 20th of the preceding month.

Unlucky, upon the whole, as Carl VI had been in the wars he had undertaken, he had succeeded in the great enterprise of his reign, namely in having, on the failure of male heirs to the German branch of the Hapsburg family (through the death of his infant son, Leopold, November 4, 1716), his eldest daughter recognized by Europe as the inheritress of the family titles, powers, dignities and what not—i.e., the right of succession confirmed to a female—and thus Maria Theresa became the head of the Austrian monarchy.

She and her sister, Maria Anna, had for husbands Franz and Carl, sons of Leopold Joseph, duke of Lorraine—the elder, Franz, taking that title in due course, adding to it that of Grand Duke of Tuscany, and, after the death of Carl VII, becoming by election, Franz I, Emperor of Germany.

The two archduchesses had been thoroughly trained in music—strange if they had not been—by Wagenseil on the harpsichord, and by Naucini in singing. We have already seen their names as vocalists in many of the pieces above named. In 1739, while in Florence as Grand Duchesses of Tuscany, Maria Theresa sang a duet with the castrato Senesino, who after the break-down of the two Italian operas in London, had returned to Italy and, according to the reports of that day, her part was executed in such style as to draw tears from the old eunuch's eyes. Tears from the eyes of him—the cunning, revengeful old Italian—who had just come from his pleasant work of aiding in Handel's ruin—do not infallibly prove that the reigning princess was indeed a very great songstress—but there is proof enough from other sources that she did both her masters honor. Maria Theresa's accession to the thrones guaranteed to her by the pragmatic sanction, she being then but twenty-three and a half years old, was the signal for the Elector of Bavaria, the King of Poland, the Elector of Saxony, the King of Spain, and above all, [Thomas] Nutshell Carlyle's spotless, honorable and high-minded hero, Friedrich II of Prussia, to invade and seize her territories. She had little time for music during those first years of her reign, engaged publicly in defending her realms, attacked thus from all sides, and privately with her almost annual infant. For she gave to Austria an archduke or archduchess in 1737, '38, '39, '41, '42, '43, '45, '46, '47, '48, '50, '51, '52, '54, '55, and '56, in all sixteen, several of whom, however, died in infancy.

Hence the first festive performance noted by "B---r," which belongs to this article, was on January 8, 1744, upon occasion of the marriage of the archduchess Maria Anna to Carl Alexander of Lorraine. *Ipermestra,* musical drama in three acts, with dances. Text by Metastasio, music by Hasse and Holzbauer (ballet). Metastasio says of it, "Esecuto da grandi e distinti personaggi a loro privatissimo trattenimento; ma poi rappresentato da musici e cantatrici nel gran Teatro di Corte." (Executed by great and distinguished personages for their own most private entertainment, but afterwards by the singers and songstresses upon the great court stage.)

1749. *La danza,* a cantata for two voices; text Metastasio, music Bonno; sung for the first time in the presence of Franz and Maria Theresa, by a lady and gentleman of the court.

Same year, November. *Augurio di Felicità,* festive piece, at Schönbrunn—same authors—for the name-day of Elisabeth, Maria Theresa's mother; sung by her (the latter's) daughters, Maria Anna, Christina and Elisabeth, aged respectively eleven, seven and six years.

1750, October 15. *La rispettosa tenerezza,* a dramatic sketch—text, Metastasio; music, Reutter—sung on Maria Theresa's name-day, by the same three young archduchesses.

This Reutter is the same who brought Joseph Haydn a few years before from the country to sing in the imperial chapel.

1751, April. *Il re pastore,* musical drama, three acts; text, Metastasio; music, Bonno; performed in Schönbrunn by the nobility.

1752. *L'eroe cinese,* musical drama, three acts, same authors, on the birthday festival of the Empress at Schönbrunn, by young gentlemen and ladies of the court.

1754, September 24. *Le Cinesi,* dramatic piece, Metastasio, music, Gluck; performed at Schlosshof, residence of the prince of Sachsen-Hilburghausen, during a visit of the Emperor and Empress there. The ballet in the piece was danced by two of the young archduchesses and a lady of the court.

1754, December. *La corona, tributo di rispetto e d'amore;* text, Metastasio; music, Reutter. Birthday of Emperor Franz, sung by three of his daughters.

1755, May 5. *La danza,* dramatic sketch by Metastasio and Gluck—introduction to a ballet danced by the ladies of the court, sung by the famous Caterina Gabrielli and a Signora Friberth at the summer palace of Laxenburg, near Vienna.

1755. *La Gara,* dramatic sketch, same authors, on occasion of the birth of Marie Antoinette (November 2), in the Empress' private apartments, sung by archduchess Marianna and two ladies.

1756. *Il re pastore* again.

1757. *Il sogno,* dramatic sketch, Metastasio and Reutter, in the private rooms of the Empress, by Marianna and two ladies.

1762. *Atenaïde, ovvero gli affetti generosi,* dramatic sketch, by Metastasio and Bonno, written for and rehearsed by five daughters of Maria Theresa, but the performance was prevented by the illness of Elisabeth.

1764. *Egeria,* dramatic festive piece by Metastasio and Hasse, performed, on occasion of archduke Joseph's being crowned King of Rome, by four of his sisters. His brother, Leopold, now seventeen years old (afterwards his successor as Emperor) danced the part of Cupid.

1765, January 23. *Il Parnasso confuso,* dramatic piece by Metastasio and Gluck. This was performed in Schönbrunn, during the festivities on occasion of Joseph's marriage with the Bavarian princess, Theresa Josepha, by his sister Maria Elisabeth (Apollo); Maria Amalia, afterwards Duchess of Parma; Maria Josepha, afterwards Queen of the Sicilies; and Maria Caroline, afterwards the notorious Queen of Naples (three muses). [But Gerber differs from "B---r" in the notice of this piece.]

Same year, *La corona,* by Metastasio and Gluck, was rehearsed by four of Maria Theresa's daughters (all soprani), but the sudden death of their father, Franz I on August 18, prevented the performance.

Everybody who has read Austrian history of that period, knows how the Empress took the death of her husband to heart, and no one can be surprised that with *La corona,* "B---r's" list closes.

♯ ♯ ♯ ♯ ♯

Seventeen hundred and sixty-five! Handel, who for a generation towered as grandly above all contemporary composers of Italian opera, as now for three generations he has above all composers of oratorio, had been dead some six years. Mozart was a child of nine years, astonishing the musical world by his precocity. Joseph Haydn was almost overwhelmed with the multifarious duties of Kapellmeister to Prince Esterházy—a position he had now filled for five years; and Gluck, while composing regular Italian operas for the imperial stage, had three years before (April 5, 1762) produced one shockingly irregular—*Orpheus and Eurydice*—but which of all up to that time, by any composer, is the only one now [1863] to be heard.

Joseph II, twenty-four years old in 1765, and associated with his mother in the government, can hardly be expected amid the cares and duties of State to learn music anew, or to give up at once the school in which he has been educated for one which did not yet exist—and which was not really developed until the child Mozart had become a man, twenty years later.

And in 1766, young Antonio Salieri arrived in Vienna.

CHAPTER 2

Salieri's Early Years in Italy

A HUNDRED YEARS AGO and more, Signor Salieri was a well-to-do shopkeeper or trader in the fortified town of Legnago, in the Venetian territory. He must have had a taste for music, for he gave his son, Francesco, the means of becoming a good pianist, but, more than that, put him under the great Tartini to study the violin, upon which he became a distinguished player.

Antonio was born on August 19 [actually the 18th], 1750, and as soon as he was old enough was sent to the public school to learn Latin, and put under his brother, Francesco, to study violin, pianoforte and singing. In process of time Giuseppe Simoni, organist in the Cathedral at Legnago and pupil of the famous Padre Martini of Bologna, became his musical instructor.

Francesco was often employed at the church festivals in and about Legnago, to play the violin concerto—a common feature in the service on such occasions. The best musicians of the neighborhood usually assembled to take part, and thus the saint's celebration became a musical festivity. Little Antonio was, from his infancy, passionately fond of music, and when there was room in the carriage which took his brother to and from the place of his engagement, he was allowed to accompany him. When he was ten years old, on such an occasion there was no room for him, but since the village was not far from home, he started off on foot without asking permission of his parents who subsequently suffered no small anxiety at his long absence.

Upon his return with his brother at night, the angry father threatened him with confinement in his room, and bread and water for a week upon a repetition of the offense. The boy, at first greatly frightened, thought the matter over and concluded

25

that it was not so very bad after all. He was such a full-blooded boy that he had been taught to drink nothing but water, and remained a water-drinker all his life; perhaps this was the reason for his extraordinary fondness for all sorts of sugar preparations and sweet dishes for which he was noted in Vienna. According to his own account he reasoned out his father's threat in this manner:

> "The punishment is not so very dreadful, when one can hear such beautiful music in return. I never drink wine anyway; I don't like the taste of it unless it is sweet; and as to bread, if I can only get sugar, why I would just as soon eat it with bread as anything else; and at any rate I will begin at once to lay in a little stock of sugar."

The boy had actually laid in a provision against imprisonment, by the time his brother had another engagement to which he was unable to take Antonio. Let the old man himself tell his childish experience:

> "This time I saw my brother drive off with great indifference, as I supposed, and remained quietly at home. After half an hour or so—it was still early in the morning and my parents, brothers and sisters were not yet up—I told a servant girl that I would go to mass, and really did leave the house for that purpose. Quite involuntarily, and contrary to my custom, I selected a more distant church, and one which stood near the city gate through which my brother had been driven to the village church-festival. After service, I came out of the church really intending to return home when the thought struck me that that village also was not far from the town. I stood and said to myself: 'My disobedience cannot be so very great a fault, as I am only guilty of it for the sake of hearing sacred music.' Thinking the matter over in this way, my longing for this, as it seemed to me, innocent pleasure, increased, and believing myself unobserved, off I started on the road to the festival. But this time I failed in my reckoning. A person, whom my father had set upon the watch, overtook me when hardly through the city gate, stopped me, and led me back home. 'Thus you obey me?' cried my father,

angrily, 'and thus you have forgotten the punishment I threatened? Away to your chamber and get ready for a good dinner.' I sneaked away to my room like a bird to its cage after a warm bath, and father locked me in. But, as my head was full of the idea that I had not committed any heinous crime, I was not much cast down; and having a good breakfast with my brother in the morning before he drove off, I was not hungry, so I set myself now to a book, and now to the pianoforte, and waited for the dinner hour, curious to see if my father would really carry out his threat. The hour struck, and sure enough, the next moment the servant came and brought me a piece (not so very large) of bread, a bottle of water and a glass. After the ugly old woman had placed them all before me, she went out of the room with an ill-boding smile and locked the door again. Well, I saw now that my father was really resolved to keep his word; but the thought of my hidden treasure of sugar lessened the pain. Now I went to the clothes press where I had concealed my store to get a portion of it; I hunted and hunted, but not a trace of sugar was to be found! I had entrusted my secret to my sister; she had entrusted it to my mother, and she had *entrusted* it to my father, who on that very morning before I was brought back, had confiscated my entire stock as contraband of war.

And now, indeed, I felt the full weight of my punishment, and, as I had on other occasions learned that my father was a man of his word, the terror came upon me of being obliged to pass eight everlasting days shut up, and upon such small rations. Overcome with shame and pain I broke out into loud crying. At this moment, my father, who had been listening, opened the door, and said: 'Ah, ha, my fine gentleman, pretty tricks these of yours! disobeying my orders, hiding away sugar —what will be the end of it all?' Full of repentance I prayed forgiveness, which was granted, with the proviso that in the future, when brother Francesco went to a festival, and there was no room for me in the carriage, I

must be shut up all day in my room—a sentence which
was rigidly carried out. For this time, after this pathetic
scene, I was allowed to go to the table. But as several
friends dined there that day, and the story of the sugar
had got out, I had to put up with many a banter; indeed
for a long time afterward, when I met any one of them,
I always had to hear the question: 'Well, Tony, how are
you off for sugar?'"

An odd boy, ardently fond of music (and sugar)!

Mosel gives the following anecdote from Salieri's papers as a
proof of the feeling for difference in style and for fitness in
music with which he was born. He was walking once with his
father, when they met a monk who was the organist of his con-
vent. The boy was in the habit of attending the mass and vespers
of that church, when performed *musicaliter*, and had often heard
this monk, "in the almost universal style at that time in Italy," pre-
luding on the organ in a *scherzando*, and therefore, for the place,
improper style. The father greeted the monk and talked a few
moments with him. Tony also greeted him, but with marked
coldness which had also on other occasions attracted his father's
notice.

"Why didn't you greet the monk more respectfully?" asked the
father after they had separated.

"I would gladly greet him properly," said the boy, "but I don't
like him because he is a bad organist."

"Why, how can you, boy, judge in such matter, you, who have
hardly begun to study music?"

"True, I am only a beginner, but if I were in his place, it seems
to me, I would play the organ with more solemnity."

Before Antonio was fifteen years old he had lost, first, his
mother, and soon after his father, and misfortunes of divers
kinds had fallen upon the family, so that the children—Francesco, the violinist; another son, a monk in Padua; a third son
whose name is not even given, Antonio and two sisters—six in
all—were left almost in bitter poverty. Antonio took refuge with
the brother in Padua, where he remained until some time in the
year 1766, when a Venetian nobleman, Giovanni Mocenigo, an
old friend of his father, who had heard of the sorrows of the
Salieri family, became his protector. Mocenigo took the little

musician from his brother to Venice with the intention of sending him to Naples to acquire a thorough musical education.

One evening while in Venice, Antonio was present at the first performance of an opera, probably *Adriano in Syria.* His seat was in the parterre and hard by a box occupied by a lady who was greeted by a tall, thin man, quite enveloped in a fur cloak, standing near, also in the parterre. The tall man crowded himself before Antonio to have a chat with the lady so that the broad sleeve of his cloak rested against the boy. In course of the conversation it became clear to him that the stranger was no other than the composer of the new opera—maestro di cappella Pietro Guglielmi—who some two years later brought out his *Ezio* and other works in London.

Nothing but the absorption of his attention by the lady prevented Guglielmi from noticing with what enthusiasm the boy beside him hugged his coat sleeve to his breast out of pure reverence and love for the composer. Forty years afterwards the French National Institute had occasion to elect a corresponding member in the musical section—the deceased member was Guglielmi, his successor Antonio Salieri.

The stay of Antonio with Mocenigo in Venice lasted but some three months during which, however, he was not idle; he studied thorough bass with Giovanni Pescetti, deputy *maestro di cappella* of San Marco, and singing with Ferdinando Pacini, a tenor singer in the same Chapel, and lodger in Mocenigo's house.

One of the Carneval operas of that year (1766) at Venice was *Achille in Sciro,* libretto by Metastasio. The ballet and chamber music composer at the court of Vienna, Florian Leopold Gassmann, a native of Brux in Bohemia, was called to Italy to compose the music. Ferdinando Pacini was one of the singers employed in it, and consequently made Gassmann's acquaintance. Quite by chance he spoke to the Kapellmeister of the boy Salieri as a youth of much talent and passionately devoted to music. Gassmann was interested, desired to see him, and was so pleased with Antonio's skill, both on the pianoforte and in singing, as to beg him from Mocenigo, and take him to Vienna as his pupil in composition.

CHAPTER 3

Apprenticeship in Vienna

THUS IT HAPPENED THAT the orphan boy, instead of the proposed journey to Naples and musical studies there, entered Vienna on June 15, 1766, as the pupil of the Bohemian-German Gassmann, two months before completing his sixteenth year.

"And here," said Salieri, "I cannot pass over one circumstance which always floats in my grateful memory. The day after my arrival in the capital, my master took me into the Italian church to offer there my devotions. As we were going home he said to me, 'I thought it my duty to begin your musical education with God. Now it will depend upon you whether its results shall be good or bad; I shall at all events have done my duty.' Men of that sort are rare! I promised him eternal gratitude for all the good he should do me, and, praised be God! I have the right to boast that I honorably proved myself grateful so long as he lived and, after his death, to his family." A truth which all Vienna can confirm and which, no less than his distinguished talents, made him the object of universal respect—adds Mosel.

Gassmann, at that time having just entered his thirty-eighth year, and still a bachelor, arranged the boy's studies and divided his time in a manner which, fortunately, the pupil in later years put upon record—fortunately, for it shows why "there were giants in those days," to use the Old Testament phrase, or rather how those whom nature intended as such, reached their full development. It must not be forgotten that the pupil had already conquered the ordinary difficulties of the pianoforte, the violin, and singing—the reading of music being a matter of course—and had had instruction in thorough bass. At this point Gassmann took him in charge, the end aimed at being the mas-

30

tery of vocal—especially operatic—composition.

Antonio was at once provided with a master in the German and French languages, and a priest, Don Pietro Tommasi, gave him lessons in Latin, Italian, poetry, and other branches of knowledge which bore upon the science of his future profession. All these teachers gave him daily instruction. With a young Bohemian whose name seems to have escaped Salieri's memory, he continued his studies in thorough bass, in the reading of scores, and the violin. At the same time, Gassmann himself began to teach him counterpoint. To make his progress in this branch—better to say, in the very foundation of the art of composition—more easy and rapid, Tommasi was directed to devote a part of every Latin lesson to the translation of a passage from Fux's *Gradus ad Parnassum,* that celebrated work which Gassmann made the basis of his system of instruction.

Mosel, the mutilator of Handel's works, a man whose name one cannot bear with patience when one thinks of his editions of *Samson* and *Belshazzar* (God save the mark!)—*Samson* with the entire part of Harapha, the Philistine giant, omitted—this I.F. Edler von Mosel, infinite ass as he was in some points, had also some good ideas. And here is one of them. "One sees," says he, "with what zeal, circumspection, and at the same time adaptation to the end proposed, Salieri's musical education was arranged and conducted. The disciples of art in those days did not gain the title of composer so cheaply as now, when every one, as soon as he knows that two pure fifths or octaves must not follow each other immediately, believes himself a master of composition, and that all other branches of knowledge, which a real and worthy composer considers indispensably necessary, are superfluous, and the study of them as mere loss of time."[1]

One of Gassmann's sternest commands was that his pupil should confine himself entirely to his study of the rules in his music; but the latter's longing to compose was irresistible, and when alone, he gave way to it, now writing an instrumental and then a vocal piece, as it happened, composing his own text for the latter. These pieces he carefully hid in his bed, to enjoy at leisure, but they were discovered and his master gave him a

[1] Few signs of progress in our American music are so encouraging, as the fact that Harvard can count so many of her sons devoted to music in some form or another.—A.W.T.

severe reprimand and forbade him, without special permission, to take note paper from his room—he was not yet ripe for composition. Salieri took care to obey in the matter of the note paper, but the injunction to confine himself, for the present, exclusively to the grammatical rules of music he very soon forgot, and every bit of white paper he could lay his hands on was immediately ruled with staves and filled with his musical ideas, good, bad or indifferent.

♯ ♯ ♯ ♯ ♯

Let him go on composing and disobeying his master for a time while we endeavor to put ourselves into the time and place in which the youth so singularly found himself instead of being among Italians enjoying the exquisite beauties of Naples and the musical advantages then so numerous there.

Maria Theresa lost her husband, Emperor Franz I, on August 18, 1765, and never entered the theater but once afterward, at the performance of Diderot's *Father of a Family* [*Le Père de famille*] in 1771. The Imperial theaters remained closed after Franz's death some eight months, during which divers changes were determined upon and effected by the new Emperor of Germany, Joseph II, who also shared with his mother the administration of the hereditary dominions.

The French troupe of actors was dismissed to the great dissatisfaction of the court-theater public; the management was given up by the Court, and the two theaters—that near the *Kärntner Tor* (Carinthian gate) and that attached to the *Burg* (the Palace)—were leased. It is not our purpose to speak of the excessively low condition of the spoken drama at that time in Vienna and how, through the influence of French actors and English dramas, it rose to be the first in Germany. Suffice it that there were three parties, one for extemporized plays, i.e., the plan of a drama given, the dialogue extemporized by the actors; a second for regular pieces; and the third for a French company. The lessee, Hilverding, opened the houses on Easter Monday, 1776, but gave way very soon to a Mr. Häring and two companions, who in turn transferred them to Affligio on May 10, 1767, who engaged a French troupe again.

Joseph II seems to have labored all his life under the misfortune of a disposition to begin great things and drive them only as long as the novelty lasted; thus it was with the founding of a national drama now and of a national opera some years later, and so the French drama came again upon the boards.

"And now a word more upon Joseph the Second." So begins an article in the Speyer *Musikalische Correspondenz* (July 28, 1790), which article is precisely to the point and is confirmed by the hundred other authorities which need not be cited.

"As in many an instance," says our writer, "in the matter of State economy, he had the ill luck to be misled by a sort of

Emperor Joseph II (1741-1790)

deceptive polish in the selection of persons who should help him
in carrying his noble ideas into practice, precisely so it happened
to him in music. If there as any one person in our imperial capital who prized and loved music, and at the same time understood it, it was he. Every afternoon he enjoyed the pleasure of
performing in a little concert with three of his chamber musicians and his chamberlain, [Johann Kilian] Strack, who possessed his master's implicit confidence, and was also a musician.
But rarely was the choice of pieces such as it might and ought to
have been. You understand what I mean by this. Salieri, our worthy Salieri it is true, was his idol, but then the position of a
Kapellmeister at the head of his orchestra in the opera is very
different from that in the private apartment of his ruler. There
he has full liberty of action; but here, where the constellations
are very different, it is possible that even a hint from one of
his subalterns must be obeyed as a command. But further, the
first violinist in these private concerts of the Emperor was
[Franz] Kreibich[2]—a man created to direct music, and one who
has a fine knowledge of its theory but, to his misfortune as an
artist, also a little of a charlatan, perhaps more affected than real.
His moral character good, etc., etc.* * * The chamberlain,
Strack, played the violoncello and had also care of the musical
library. It would carry me too far to draw you a picture of the
moral character of this man. You know this sort of people who,
as Schiller says, are the makeshifts, where numbers are few, in a
moment make themselves seven times short, and seven times
long, like a butterfly on a pin and have to keep a register of
their master's.... Enough, Strack was always about Joseph and
knew so well how to take advantage of his opportunities as to be
able to do everything he had a mind to in musical matters.

"Waborzil, cabinet musician and director in the theater, [was]
a very good violinist, but a most mediocre director. It lies in his
character, except when forced by the duties of his place, to do
nothing at all for art and he composes nothing. Hoffmann and
Bonnheimer were formerly cabinet musicians in the service of
Archduke Maximilian, Joseph's brother and, from 1784, Archbishop and Elector of Cologne.

[2] Thayer calls him Kriebig.—T.A.

"On extra occasions [Ignaz] Umlauf, who has now the charge of musical lessons of the royal children [Leopold's, Joseph's successor—A.W.T.], and whom the Emperor Joseph raised from being a viola player to the place of Kapellmeister, because his opera *Die Bergknappen* had the luck to please him wonderfully even though it was received by many with but doubtful applause.

"Finally, I mention a certain Krottendorfer, a man who gained Strack's good will by flattery and obeyed his every wish like a puppet.

"All these persons met together only in extraordinary cases. Usually only three of them with Strack and Joseph. The latter took often the pianoforte, often the violoncello, and not seldom a vocal part. Very rarely were quartets played and when they were, none but such as Kreibich or Strack had recommended as palatable dishes. Why these gentlemen so carefully excluded a Haydn, Mozart, Kozeluch, Pleyel and other fine musicians, together with their works, I leave here unanswered. Enough that Joseph was not allowed to hear a note of these certainly excellent composers; on the other hand, all the more from such as are not worthy to unloose the latches of their shoes. The Emperor was fond of the pathetic and sometimes had music by Gassmann, Ordonez, etc., placed on the stands. Generally, however, favorite passages from serious operas and oratorios were played from the score. Joseph had the fault of greatly enjoying it when the music went at odds and ends; and the more Kreibich labored and heated himself and stormed, the more heartily Joseph laughed. These imperial concerts therefore had often a double object, that of artistic enjoyment and of sport. Kreibich played in them the part for which in old times it was the custom to appoint a certain class of persons, that of butt for their wit. Kreibich was also really a man to bear a jest and joke if one did not forget at every stroke to add a few drops of the universal balsam called flattery.

"This private concert took place daily in the Emperor's own room. It began for the most part immediately after his dinner and lasted until time for the play. If public business interfered, it began later and lasted so much the longer, especially when nothing of interest was given in the theaters. Strack was always present but the three other chamber musicians took turns, three today, other three tomorrow. The Emperor visited the theater very constantly, especially the Italian opera in which he took great pleasure. Salieri's *Axur, Re d'Ormus* was his favorite.

"You see that he would have done much for music if happily he had chosen a different set of musicians. Salieri, no doubt, saw the real state of the case. But, as I said before, the relations of a Kapellmeister in the public concert-room are very different from those in the cabinet of a Joseph. Salieri had too much policy to come into collision with the *shadows* of his Monarch, and the others must hold it a favor to enjoy their positions with the finger on their lips."

It will be noticed that the above was written after Joseph's decease and describes the confirmed habits of his later years. He was born on March 13, 1741, and had consequently completed his 25th year only three months before the boy Salieri was brought to Vienna.

He, like his ancestors, had received a thorough musical education with a bias to the Italian Operatic School, which as yet had no rival but in the French comic opera, and this rivalry was little felt in Vienna though a few years later, nay even now, it had the upper hand in North and West Germany where Parisian pieces were translated and given everywhere. Joseph played various instruments well, was a master of singing, and read scores with facility. Another writer says of the private concerts described above that they followed his dinner (which he ate alone in his music room, giving hardly more than fifteen minutes to it) and lasted about an hour, in which he played viola or violoncello, or the pianoforte, in which latter case he sang a part. He took great interest in the *opera buffa*, selected the pieces to be performed, looked them through in those private concerts with his brother, Maximilian, and attended the rehearsals in the theater.

It was therefore natural that when Affligio took the theaters in hand he should devote himself to the French spoken drama, the ballet and the Italian *opera buffa* to the utter neglect of the German stage for which Joseph's zeal had, for the present, cooled, and which existed, one may almost say, only in the form of local burlesque pieces and farces. We have nothing to do here with the history of the German spoken drama in Vienna, which soon after began to rise, and in a dozen or fifteen years reached remarkable perfection—not even with the energetic and indefatigable labors of Sonnenfels, a name of high honor in theatrical annals.

Divers changes in the management took place, but in August 1770, the two theaters came into the hands of Count Kohary, with Franz Heufeld, a dramatic writer of some note, as manager. That such a position was no sinecure, see the following: there was a German and a French company for the spoken drama, an Italian opera (*seria* and *buffa*), and a very costly ballet under Noverre. The Italian operas were performed once a week in the *Kärntnertor* house, and twice a week in the *Burg*. The troupe consisted of eight male solo singers and seven women soloists. The expenses reached 30,275 florins, some $15,000 [in 1864 dollars]. The serious operas given were not numerous, and confined almost to those of Gluck and, in time, of Salieri; but the lists of performances in those years show comic operas by Galuppi, Gassmann, Guglielmi, Paisiello, Piccini, Salieri, and, by and by, Righini.

Ballets were given daily in both theaters(?); Noverre directed in both, but those of the *Burg* (the French) far surpassed those in the *Kärntnertor* (German). In the *Burg* there were five solo female dancers, ten men, ten women, and sixteen pupils in the corps de ballet. The ballet expenses reached 50,000 florins. The two orchestras cost 15,000 florins. Gassmann was Kapellmeister and composer; Starzer composed for the ballets; Trani was director of the orchestra in the *Burg*, which numbered thirty-one members—in the other house but twenty-six.

Gluck, at the time of Salieri's advent with Gassmann, had produced only one of the works which was to live and keep his name alive when the others above recorded are forgotten, *Orpheus and Eurydice* (1764); *Alceste* was, however, soon to follow (1768).[3]

# # # # #

This much seemed necessary to give the reader even a faint picture of the scene and actors in the quiet drama in which we

---

[3] The visit of Dr. Burney to Vienna fell in these years (1772), and to those who have access to his *Present State of Music in Germany,* I recommend the reading of the last half of Volume I. —A.W.T.

are to make the young Salieri our principal character—and to whom we now come back.

Gassmann, who had been called to Vienna as ballet composer in 1762, had become quite a favorite of the young Emperor, had been appointed chamber composer and three times a week was one of those who aided in the private concerts above described. Joseph learned in some manner soon after the return of the composer from Venice, that he had brought a very promising youth with him, and expressed a desire to see him. Gassmann, of course, took his pupil to the palace where he was very kindly received by the Emperor who addressed him with: "Ah, good morning, how are you pleased with Vienna?"

Salieri, frightened, embarrassed, and accustomed in Venice to the title of Excellency, replied: "Well, your Excellency!" and instantly added by way of correcting his mistake: "Extraordinarily well, your Majesty!"

Some of the musicians of the chapel laughed at the boy's embarrassment and simplicity: but Joseph went on asking him about his home, his family and so on, and Antonio, having fully recovered himself, answered all questions with great discretion, and embraced the opportunity to express to the Emperor his gratitude toward Gassmann, who was of course present, and whom he represented as his benefactor and second father. Joseph then required him to sing and play something from memory, which he did quite to the satisfaction of the monarch. Now began the ordinary chamber concert, of which the music that day happened to be vocal pieces from Hasse's opera *Alcide al bivio*. Salieri sang not only the alto in the choruses, but several solos with ease and correctness at sight from the score. This pleased Joseph much and he ordered Gassmann always in the future to bring his pupil with him; this he did, and so began Salieri's service at the Imperial Court, never to be interrupted so long as his powers lasted.

As a practical school, one in which the youth should learn the application of theoretical rules and forms, which at home he had studied in books and scores, Gassmann took his pupil regularly to the theater. The master directed a new piece only three times, after which Salieri was put at the spinet or harpsichord—for the pianoforte was not as yet in the theater, nor had the old mode of directing from a keyed instrument (kept up in the London Philharmonic concerts long after it had disappeared almost everywhere else) given way to the only true one—since the growth of the modern orchestra—that of a conductor, with his baton, standing or seated, elevated above his forces.

Of the mass of anecdotes and reminiscences which Salieri wrote down in his latter years, Mosel has given a few at length, which are characteristic both of the man—as a youth engaging in adventures and frolics, and as the old man recalling them to mind with evident satisfaction—and of the scenes in which he lived; they are therefore worth repeating.

On one of the first three evenings of some new piece, the music of which pleased him as little as did the public, instead of remaining in his place in the pit to listen to the musical effects—as Gassmann demanded of him—Salieri gave way to a desire to go upon the stage. He found the machinists at work behind a drop curtain preparing the table for a grand supper to come off in the next scene. Their work was done, but the youth stopped a moment to look at the *papier maché* pastries, capons, etc., when—*potz tausend!*—the prompter's whistle for change of scene sent up the curtain, and, not to be seen crossing the stage by all the people, and still worse, by his master, the poor boy had to pop under the table—a movement executed without being seen. Now came the actors and seated themselves singing at the table to feast upon their *papier maché*. There was plenty of room for Antonio to remain without touching anyone and, as the scene closed the act, he was comparatively unconcerned, thinking himself safe enough from being discovered by anyone, save perhaps a machinist or two. But one of the supperless supper eaters had to drop his napkin, and stooping to pick it up had to see something black in the darkness caused by the low hanging tablecloth; and had to take that something black to be a great dog—and, at a pause in the music, had to tell his neighbor of the discovery—and his neighbor had to pass the news along, so that in two minutes the four men and four women at the table all had to know about the great black dog, and one of the women had to be terribly afraid of cats and dogs, and she had to spring up with

a shriek, and the small audience had to have a great laugh—and
poor Antonio was there half dead with anxiety and fright—all
because an actor happened to drop his napkin. However, the
music went on, the dog was found to be a young man, the frightened songstress was relieved, and sat down again, laughing, to
the *papier maché,* and so the act came to a close. No sooner was
the curtain down than Salieri sprang out, and amid a shout of
laughter explained the matter, beseeching the actors not to tell
his master, who, as he knew, would soon be upon the stage, and
hurried off to his place in the pit. In spite of Antonio's prayers,
Gassmann was told the story immediately. At the close of the play
he went into the pit as usual to get his pupil, but said not a word
about the affair. Nor at supper, nor afterwards, and the poor fellow went to bed with a lightened heart. Nor at breakfast, and
Antonio's terrible anxiety was relieved. Nor at dinner, to which
Gassmann had invited two friends, was a hint at the great black
dog. Before the group left the table, an Italian coachman (*vetturino*) entered, and said that he had been told the master
wished to speak to him.

"I have sent for you," answered Gassmann, "to learn whether
you are going back soon to Italy, as I am going to send that boy,
there, home again."

Pale and frightened, Antonio sprang up and told the whole
story, half crying, half in fun. Neither Gassmann nor his friends
could keep sober faces, and the boy was forgiven, with the proviso of stricter obedience in the future. The boy promised
and kept his promise. He learned afterwards that the scene
with the *vetturino* had been planned beforehand by his master; but even that did not efface the memory of his terrible
fright.

Until the death of Gassmann on January 22, 1774, Salieri
never received any regular salary for his services, either in the
Emperor's private concerts or in the theater; but Joseph made
him a present every New Year's Day, on the first one of fifty, on
the others of eighty ducats—the ducat being almost exactly
$2.50 [in 1864 dollars]. Considering what in those days a ducat
would buy in Vienna, then an exceedingly cheap place to live in,
the present was munificent. Antonio always placed the money in
his master's hands, who religiously used it for the youth's bene-

fit, in the purchase of clothes and the payment of his other teachers.[4]

In the large house joining and belonging to St. Michael's church opposite the Burg Theater, and up four flights of stairs, lived the family Martinez, with whom Metastasio, the poet, lodged. The father, a Neapolitan by birth, Spanish by descent, was now dead; the son an assistant librarian in the Imperial Library; the daughter, Metastasio's celebrated pupil, was the young lady at whose music lessons under Porpora, some fifteen or twenty years before, young Joseph Haydn came down from his garret overhead to play the spinet or harpsichord.

Miss Martinez played an important part in the musical social life of Vienna for many a year. Gassmann took Antonio and introduced him to Metastasio. Every Sunday morning he was there, both for the benefit to be derived from the conversation of the old poet—the most famous perhaps, except Voltaire, then living—and to make the acquaintance of the distinguished literary, scientific and artistic men, as well as others notable only for rank, who honored his Sunday receptions from 9 a.m. to 12 noon. Young Salieri soon became welcome at other times and seasons, and especially evenings, when his aid was gladly accepted in the musical performances of the family; often when they were alone, Metastasio had him read entire scenes from his works dramatically, "which," says Salieri, "was for me an excellent school in declamation—a school, which, in the opinion of Metastasio, is an indispensable necessity to anyone who will really cultivate a talent for musical vocal composition."

In those days it was thought necessary to have an education as well as genius; to develop talent as well as possess it; to have the taste refined by an acquaintance with literature and the sister

[4] Joseph Haydn had a story of his master Reutter, music-director of St. Stephan's, of another color. Time, November 14, 1748; place, Klosterneuburg, a few miles above Vienna on the Danube; occasion, festival of St. Leopold, at which the Empress Maria Theresa and her husband Franz were present. Haydn's voice—he had long been leading soprano in the St. Stephan choir—was breaking, and the Empress had recently said to Reutter: "Joseph Haydn no longer sings, he croaks." The director had consequently to select another boy for the solos, and Michael Haydn, younger brother of Joseph, was selected, who sang a *Salve Regina* so exquisitely, that the Empress and her husband each gave him twelve ducats. "Michael," asked Reutter, "what will you do with so much money?" The boy thought a moment. "Our father has just lost a beast. I will send him twelve ducats, and beg you to take care of the rest for me until my voice also breaks." Reutter took such excellent care of the money that Michael never saw it again.—A.W.T.

arts, as well as by a knowledge of the great productions in its immediate sphere; and to have the rules of harmony and counterpoint so thoroughly mastered, that the composer no more thought about them when at work, than I do of Murray's *Grammar* and Whately's *Rhetoric*[5] while scratching off this sentence. To his acquaintance with Metastasio and the instruction in declamation thus gained was due, in great measure, the great perfection of Salieri's works in echoing the sense of his texts in his music. Their real dramatic excellence was a quality which so distinguished them that Salieri, their author, was far down into our own century [i.e., the nineteenth] *the* great teacher of dramatic composition in Vienna, as Albrechtsberger was of the theory of music.

In the year 1768, the pupil began to hear specimens of his compositions performed in public. Gassmann, having charge of the Italian opera, often had slight changes, additions and the like, to make in the music, and these he occasionally entrusted to his pupil, mainly to put a stop to his constant entreaties to be allowed to produce something in public. That the pupil often composed texts, already set by his master, for the purpose of self-improvement—as the boy Benjamin Franklin re-wrote Steele's and Addison's *Spectators*—Gassmann did not know.

One of his tricks at that time which ended happily is a good indication of his character, and, when an old fellow, he evidently heartily enjoyed the memory of the success of the young one.

They had an old spinet in the theater which was moved from the orchestra to the rehearsal room and back, as it was needed in rehearsal or at performance, and was so superannuated as not to remain in tune even for a single evening. The singers complained, too, that they could not hear the accompaniment, and Salieri found it alike useless to play in the higher or lower octaves. Here a string snapped, there one gave way; here some of the quills, which snapped the strings, were lacking; there they remained sticking above the strings. In short, the old thing, already nearly useless, grew worse each day, and the manager was too miserly to buy a new one.

One morning after a rehearsal at which Salieri's martyrdom

---

[5] Like Whelpley's *Compend of History,* these were popular textbooks in Thayer's youth, each running through numerous editions.—T.A.

had been almost intolerable, he was obliged to wait for a copyist to make certain corrections in the parts, and found himself quite alone with his enemy. He threw the old instrument wide open, mounted a chair beside it and jumped bodily. What havoc with the internal organism this kind of performance would make, may be safely left to the imagination.

When the copyist came the spinet was, as usual, closed and locked, and Salieri was calmly busy in his corrections of the score, which the other was to transfer to the parts. All the directions were given as usual and the two left the room together. That evening was an opera, so the spinet was transferred from the hall to the orchestra, and an hour before the performance the tuner came to perform his daily task. He opened it; "Mercy on us!" and sank back into the chair. He called the men who had brought it down. They were as overcome by the sad sight as the tuner himself. They hurried off to call Gassmann and the manager, and while they were seeking for a clue to the criminal, another instrument for that evening was brought in. Next day another rehearsal, at which the spinet was thoroughly examined; nearly all the strings were gone, and the sounding board itself crushed—the career of that spinet was ended.

"The cover must have tumbled in," said one.

"No, a music-stand," said a second.

"Not so," said the tuner, "all together would not have done so much damage; some devil or other must have jumped into it."

"The good man has almost guessed it," thought Salieri, who stood by, and not too much at his ease, though no one suspected—at least seemed to suspect—him, and who was not free from anxiety until he heard Gassmann say:

"Be it as it may! Thank Heaven, the manager will at length be compelled to get a new instrument made." And so he was.

Such time as the young man could command from his various studies and duties he zealously employed in composition; and he remembered in later days as products of these essays, several little cantatas for a solo voice and thorough bass; divers pieces of church music; namely, a short mass *a cappella,* a *Salve Regina,* and several *Graduales* and Offertoires with full orchestra; a short Italian opera for four voices and chorus; six string quartets; two symphonies for orchestra; some pieces for wind instruments, and the pieces above mentioned which his master allowed him to write for the theater, which consisted of ariettas, duets, trios, some ballet movements, and trivial operatic last act finales to which in those days, very much as now, no audience paid any attention. Salieri remembered in his old age, how at that time he had no little self-satisfaction and secret pride at his share in any successful piece; would pass sleepless nights and unhappy days when such a piece was damned. What a dust we make, said the fly. Of all this preparatory work nothing was preserved except such pieces as proved available for other compositions of a later date; the rest he destroyed.

Let him tell his own story of the first of his operas which came upon the stage—if it be rather long, it is interesting, characteristic, and gives us another glimpse into the operatic life of Vienna near the close of 1769, when the youthful composer had just entered his 20th year.

"My master, Gassmann, was called to Rome at that time to compose a tragic opera for the Carneval (1770). I remained behind in Vienna to conduct the rehearsals under Vice Kapellmeister Ferandini. Giovanni Gastone Boccherini, a dancer in the Vienna opera house, a passionate lover of the art of poetry (brother of composer Luigi) had with the aid of Calzabigi (author of several excellent opera texts, among which are *Alceste* and *Orpheus*), written a comic Italian opera libretto entitled *Le donne letterate,* which was intended for Kapellmeister Gassmann. Calzabigi advised him to give it to me, for I was a beginner in composition as he [Boccherini] was in poetry and I could therefore the more easily come to an understanding with him. One morning, therefore, Boccherini came to me and, after the usual greeting, asked without the slightest preface: 'Would you like to set a comic opera text, which I have written, to music?' I answered coolly, 'Why not?' And then he told me honestly what his intention had been and how Calzabigi had advised him. Aha! thought I, so they think you able to compose opera! Courage then—we'll not let the opportunity pass unused. So I impatiently asked the poet to explain to me the plot of his opera, and to lay the text before me. Done; and after we had distributed the parts according to the powers of the company as it then was, Boccherini said: 'I will leave you now; in the meantime you can examine the text, and if you wish for changes here and there for the sake of the musical effect, when I come again, we will undertake to make them together.'

"Now I was alone again, and I locked my door, and with glowing cheeks—as was generally the case with me in later years when I had undertaken a work with real joy and delight—I read the poem through again, found it certainly well adapted to music, and, having read the vocal pieces for the third time, my first step was—as I had seen my master do—to determine which key would suit the character of each separate piece. As it drew near noon, and I consequently could not hope to begin my composition before dinner, I employed the remaining hour to go through the poem once more. I had already begun to think out the melodies for certain passages, when Madame Gassmann (for my master had married before this time) had me called to dinner. All during dinner time my opera text did not once leave my head, and I have never been able since to remember what I ate that day.

"After dinner, as I had been accustomed to do from my childhood, I, with a book in my hand, took a nap; then I took my daily walk on the walls of the city,[6] and turned back to my lodgings, full of secret pride at the confidence shown in me; I told the maid—as I had also done in the forenoon—to turn away any possible visitor, under the pretence that I was not at home. The good-natured old woman, to whom no doubt the self-important look of the commonly so jovial young gentleman and this repeated injunction seemed rather odd, looked at me quite astonished, and could not help a half-suppressed smile. But I said to myself: 'Let the poor simpleton laugh, and we will think how to do ourself credit.'

"As soon as I was alone, I felt an irrepressible desire to set the music of the introduction to the opera. I therefore sought to place the character and the situation of the persons of the drama vividly before my imagination, and suddenly discovered a movement of the orchestra which seemed to me fitted to bear up and give unity to the vocal music which the text necessarily made fragmentary. Now I fancied myself in the pit listening to the production of my ideas; they seemed to me characteristic; I wrote them down, put them again to proof, and as I was satisfied with them went on. So in half an hour the outline of the Introduction stood there on the music paper. Who was happier than I! It was now six o'clock in the evening and dark. I had lights brought. Before

---

[6] The last two bastions of those walls are today disappearing; January 1864—A.W.T.

twelve o'clock, I determined, thou goest not to bed; thy fancy is inflamed—that fire must be utilized. I read the first finale, which, as to the words, began very much like the Introduction; I read it again, formed a plan of the rhythm and keys suited to the work as whole—giving three hours to this work, but without writing a note. I felt myself weary and my cheeks burned; so I paced my room up and down, and soon again was drawn to my writing desk where I began my outline and, when midnight came, had made such progress that I laid myself in bed in high enjoyment.

"My head had been all day long too full of music and poetry not to have it also in my dreams. In fact I did hear in dreams a singular harmony, but at such a wide distance and so confused, that it caused me more pain than pleasure and finally awoke me. It was only four o'clock a.m., but all I could do, I could not again get to sleep. So I lighted my candles, looked through all I had sketched with a lead pencil the day before, went on with my outline, and had got half through the first finale when the clock struck eight, and to my surprise my poet entered the room. He could hardly believe that in so short a time I had sketched the entire introduction and half of the first finale. I played what I had written to him on the pianoforte; he was uncommonly pleased, embraced me, and really seemed not less delighted than I was myself. In short, keeping at work, with no diminution of my enthusiasm, within four weeks a good two-thirds of the opera was written out in score and orchestrated. My intention was to complete it at once but not have it performed until my master's return home from Rome and his correction of my work. But circumstances gave another turn to the matter.

"The manager had just then brought out a new opera which displeased his public and he was therefore forced to replace it with something else new. Boccherini, without saying a word to me, had told Calzabigi that I was pretty well on with my opera. He, a friend of the manager, desired to have a sort of rehearsal of what was already finished. He invited me, and I, without guessing at the real object, took my finished pieces and went with my poet. I was rather taken aback at finding there the manager, the Kapellmeister Gluck and Scarlatti;[7] but, supposing they were

[7] The three famous Scarlattis were Alessandro of Naples (1660-1725); his son, Domenico (1685-1757) and Domenico's son Giuseppe or Joseph (ca. 1718-1777). Joseph is the one here referred to.—A.W.T.

there only out of curiosity, their presence gave me uncommon pleasure. I sang and played what was finished, and in the concerted pieces Gluck and Scarlatti sang with me. Gluck, who had always liked and encouraged me, showed himself at the very beginning satisfied with my work; Scarlatti, who from time to time pointed out little grammatical errors in my composition, praised also each number on the whole and, at the close, both masters said to the manager that if I would immediately finish the lacking numbers, they could without delay rehearse and produce the work, 'in that,' in Gluck's own words, 'this work contains what is sufficient to give the public pleasure.'

"Who can imagine the joyful surprise which these words gave me, through which I instantly saw the object of the meeting. Full of confidence— *'superbo di mi stesso'*—I promised my judges the greatest industry until the work was put upon the stage. I wrote day and night, ran to the rehearsals, went through the vocal parts with the singers, corrected the copyists, joined the poet in devising the costumes and decorations, and lived in such an unbroken strain both of mental and physical powers, that if study, drudgery and sweat did not throw me upon a sick bed, I can only think it was because my happiness acted as a protection.

"The general rehearsal took place the day before the first performance. That evening I went into the theater with beating heart to hear my opera announced for the performance which was done in these words: 'Tomorrow the Italian operatic company will have the honor to produce a "new opera entitled *Le donne letterate*," poem by Herr Gastone Boccherini, music by Herr Antonio Salieri; the first work of both.' Several persons in the audience applauded which gave me sweet confidence and seemed to me a good augury. Next morning, early as I thought it possible that the bills could be posted at the street corners, I went out to see my name for the first time in print, which gave me deep gratification. But not satisfied with seeing it once—much as I had feared it might have been omitted from the other bills—I ran all round town to read it everywhere.

"It would be vain for me to try to depict the restless delight which filled that day down to the hour of the performance; but when that struck the joy changed to fear; my cheeks glowed until my whole face was scarlet, and so with faltering step I went to the instrument. As I entered the orchestra there was applause which in some degree recalled my courage. I bowed to the public, seated myself with some equanimity at the spinet, and the opera began. It gained much applause, but certainly more for the sake of encouraging the young author, who was well known, than on account of the worth of the opera. When the performance was over and I had embraced my poet, I hurried away to mix with the audience as it left the theater and hear the opinions expressed.

"'The opera is not bad,' said one. 'It pleased me right well,' said a second (that man I could have kissed). 'For a pair of beginners, it is no small thing,' said the third. 'For my part,' said the fourth, 'I found it very tedious.'

"At these words I struck off into another street for fear of hearing something still worse; but hearing at that moment new praises both of poet and composer and modestly satisfying myself with them, I returned to my lodging heated and tired, but full of joy and peace."

So ends Salieri's story. Whoever does not like it (or has no taste for the old man's simple reminiscence of his youth) had better pass it over.

Mosel says this firstling of Salieri has nowhere traces of a beginner's uncertain hand, but on the contrary, shows the value of his previous profound and indefatigable study, as well as proves his native capacity. None but those, like him, who have really prepared themselves for their art and possess an inborn talent, can thus begin their career. The work is in the old Italian style, but throughout dramatic in form, except the part of Artemia, which is devoted to *bravura* for the sake of Clementina Baglioni, who sang it and who was a concert singer with a high soprano voice; but even her part is not wanting in beautiful and expressive melody.[8] Modulations are more numerous than were then common, but in every case, says Mosel, used because called for by the dramatic situation. The arias are of the form of that day and only on this account can the work be said to be antiquated. The accompaniment is simple, the instruments employed are few, especially in the excellent comic music of both finales, so the text might easily be followed. "The opinion prevailed in those days," says Mosel, "that in the musical drama the words were of some

[8] Thus Mozart wrote the part of the Queen of Night just to show off his sister-in-law Josefa Hofer's *bravura* powers, which were a great drawing card at Schikaneder's theater, and the manager would of course have it so.—A.W.T.

importance; indeed, some composers of that time, and among them Salieri, pushed this error so far as to affirm that the poem of an opera is the main thing, and the music is added only to increase its effect and lend it that fascination which can alone arise when a melody has a real union with words. Not until our day was the brilliant discovery made that an operatic text has no other object than to yield a composer syllables for a stream of senseless tones which is again swallowed up by a still mightier flood from the orchestra."9

The tenor, Caribaldi, was one of those magnificent singers, common in the last century, if not now, from Italy, who, with splendid voice and no other instruction than what they gained simply listening to good singers, unable to distinguish one written note from another, and consequently obliged to learn every part by having it sung or played to them until it was fixed in their memories, sang with a truth, spirit, and beauty that made them more than welcome on the best stages of Europe. Caribaldi was a servant in a shop in Rome in his youth, first appeared on the stage when twenty-four years old, and came to Vienna when near thirty. The year before he had sung an aria with great applause in several theaters, which happened to be in E-flat, and thence he had drawn the conclusion that that key was specially favorable to his voice. It so happened, too, that the first opera in which he sang in Vienna was Gassmann's *L'amore artigiano* (1767), and that an aria in E-flat therein had gained him immense applause, and thus his notion had become a sort of fixed idea. Unluckily in Salieri's new opera there was no aria in that key, and the young composer was in doubt what to do. At first he took to Caribaldi only an aria in the second act which leads into a trio and left him to think that the aria in the first act was not written. "Which you will surely write in E-flat?" said the singer. "Of course," replied the other—though it was long since finished in B-flat, and there was now no time to change it. Salieri went to Domenico Poggi, another singer of the company—a good musician and friend of Caribaldi, whom he called Signor E-la-fa[10] on account of his E-flat whim—and asked what he should do.

9 A little cynical, Herr Mosel, for you are evidently speaking ironically; it is clear that you are an "old fogy," for, across the Atlantic, the people will not go to the opera unless it is an unknown tongue—and the Americans *must* be right, you know.—A.W.T.

10 See Bianca's gamut in Shakespeare's *The Taming of the Shrew*, III, i—A.W.T.

Poggi looked the aria through, saw it was good, and told him to tell the copyist to place three flats at the beginning of Caribaldi's vocal copy, for as he could not read music, if he only saw the three flats that would be sufficient. Poggi also promised to help carry on the deception, and hoped that here was an opportunity to cure his friend of his nonsense. Two days before the performance Salieri took the aria to the singer, whose eye, as the composer saw, turned immediately to the signature which was quite in order. Salieri sang the music, Caribaldi was much pleased with it, and on that day committed it to memory. Luckily for the joke, the aria was one of the pieces which received the most applause. On the second evening, when the orchestra and singers assembled on the stage before the commencement of the performance, Trani, director of the orchestra, addressed Caribaldi with: "Well now, my friend, you will no longer fancy that the key of E-flat is the only good one for you, now that you have gained such roars of applause with an aria in B-flat."

"You are joking," replied the singer. "In my part three flats stand at the beginning; hence the aria is in E-flat."

"Ha, ha! three flats for the key of B-flat!" returned Trani.

Caribaldi turned to Poggi and asked if the aria really was in B-flat.

Poggi, to carry on the joke, gravely replied by asking: "Are not three flats at the beginning?"

"Most certainly."

"Well, if that is the case, and the aria is in the major, then it must be in E-flat."

"It is in B-flat," here interposed the basso buffo, Francesco Caratoli, another great singer belonging to the company.

"No, in E-flat," persisted Poggi.

Meantime Trani had brought the score from the orchestra and showed the aria with two flats to Caribaldi, who at last began to see through the trick. At this moment Salieri, ignorant of all this, entered. Caribaldi snatched the wig from his (own) head, and threatening in pretended wrath to hurl it at the young man, cried: "Ha! thou rascally masterkin!" Salieri, guessing instantly the state of the case, fell upon one knee before him, and imitating an aria Caribaldi had recently sung in another opera both in song and action, began:

> Eccomi a'piedi tuoi.
> Mira, bell'idol mio,
> Un reo d'inanzi a te.[11]

A general laugh—the singer put on his wig again and laughed with the rest, and from that moment, as Poggi had hoped, was cured of his E-flat whim.

Salieri in this connection gives another instance of the power which these uncultivated singers gained in committing music to memory. The story is of the celebrated Brigida Banti, many years prima donna in the London Italian opera, toward the close of the last century. The last time she was in Vienna—which seems to have been about 1785—she came to Salieri and requested him to compose a Hallelujah for her to sing at some great church festival or other to which she was invited. He complied, and brought the composition to her and asked her to sing it, that he might see whether it suited her voice before he wrote out the parts for the instruments.

"Dear master," said she, "I blush to own that I hardly know the names of the notes; but as I am gifted with a good memory and some natural talent for singing, I retain very well anything which I have heard two or three times, and perform my tasks not without applause."

"You might well say," remarked Salieri, "with the *greatest* applause."

He then sang the Hallelujah. She found it splendidly adapted to her voice, and besought him to repeat it a second and a third time; the fourth time she sang it herself, not mistaking a single note. The piece was 132 bars long! Salieri could not refrain from saying:

"Madame, if I myself had not composed this piece yesterday, I should take what I have just heard for a dream." Two days afterwards she sang the piece in the church and ravished all hearers. She was the daughter of a Venetian gondolier, and began life there as the street songstress Georgi. Burney has much to say about her.

When Gassmann, some weeks later in Lent, 1770, returned from Rome, the theater being shut, the Emperor Joseph took his

[11] "Here I lie at your feet; see, my idol, a guilty culprit before you." [It seems odd, in light of Thayer's gibe at Mosel earlier, that he should provide no translation of this Italian passage, even though Mosel, p. 39, did footnote it in German.—T.A.]

young favorite's opera for one of his after-dinner concerts, that the master might hear his pupil's work, and was greatly pleased to find that Gassmann not only found no important fault against the elementary rules of composition, but was clearly very much gratified with the general tone of the single numbers, with the musical ideas, with the character of the music in general, and especially with the fitness of the musical thought to the character of the drama.

Not long after (1770), Boccherini gave Salieri the text to a pastoral opera, *L'amore innocente,* which he composed and which had great success; and the same year, a very poor text upon Don Quixote (*Don Chisciotte*), an opera in one act, with a great many dances interspersed, which was not at all to the taste of either Salieri or the public, and which failed very decidedly. Still there are some fine melodies. The music of the pastoral was afterwards used in a ballet, and no doubt the good pieces of the Don Quixote were not lost; for Salieri was as economical in the use of good ideas as Handel himself—if out of place or lost in one work, they were introduced into others.

One of those operatic subjects, which has been treated by a legion of poets and composers, both under the same and under different titles, is the story of Rinaldo and Armida in Tasso's *Jerusalem Delivered.* Salieri's fourth work for the Imperial stage was a grand opera with choruses and dances on this subject, text by Marco Coltellini,[12] composed in 1771. It was a custom of Salieri, when he had a text drawn from any historical or poetical work, as in this case, to make such work his exclusive reading while engaged in composing his text. So now the passages of Tasso, which had furnished the text of *Armida,* were read and studied to the exclusion of all else and led him, with the daring of youthful genius—he had not yet completed his twenty-first year—to write a sort of pantomime, or, as we should nowadays say, program music, for an overture. Since there was, of course, to be no scenic representation of the idea, a few words at the beginning of the libretto gave the clue to the composer's idea, and the overture was a great success.

The program was substantially this—Ubaldo's landing on Armida's Enchanted Isle being the subject: A thick fog envelopes the island; Ubaldo forces his way through; the monsters placed as

12 Thayer gives Coltellini's first name as Luigi.—T.A.

guards attack him; he puts them to flight, climbs with vast labor the cliffs and, crossing the table land, reaches at length the delicious valley which is seen when the curtain rises at the close of this overture. Mosel speaks of the principal numbers with great warmth of praise, and in relation to the closing piece, a recitative and aria of Armida, he quotes Salieri himself who says: "It is of hellish effect, of course *ad locum,* and a proper finale to an opera which is almost entirely of the diabolical sort."

Whether the young man had direct aid from the counsels of Gluck is not known; but "so much is certain," says Mosel, "that the treatment of his text, especially in the instrumented recitative, the sort of accompaniment, and the thoroughly *scenic* construction of the whole, are completely in Gluck's style; and, had he not been compelled to introduce bravura passages here and there, this *Armida,* for beauty and flow of melody, would actually deserve a higher place than that of Gluck."

Young as he was, he composed in 1772 three operas: *La fiera di Venezia,* comic opera with choruses, text by Boccherini, which had a splendid success; *Il Barone di Rocca antica,* text by Petrosellini of Rome, performed May 12, and given eighteen times that season; and *La secchia rapita,* text by Boccherini, October 21, and given ten times. Of these the third had the least success and deserved it least—the text was bad and did not fire the composer; the second belonged in the class of the really successful pieces of the day; but the first, for its excellence and for its firm hold upon the favor of the public, was the talk of old people in Vienna more than fifty years later—during which half century Mozart, Beethoven, Cherubini, and Rossini had risen upon the stage.

Salieri was now known, and so widely as to receive an invitation to the court theater in Stockholm for three years, which he rejected through the influence of Joseph.

In 1773 he composed the comic opera, *La Locandiera,* text by Domenico Poggi, after one of Goldoni's comedies—another success—with the music purposely kept subordinate to the drama, nowhere covering up the text, and with the finales almost entirely set *parlando.* This was the last of his brilliant pupil's works which Gassmann lived to hear and enjoy. He died on January 22, 1774, his wife and children finding in the grateful Salieri, so long as he lived, a fond and active protector and helper.

CHAPTER 4

Imperial Composer and Kapellmeister

T HE LOSS OF GASSMANN was a severe blow also to the young Emperor; and it was, perhaps, partly from affection to him that his favor to the Kapellmeister's pupil—almost adopted son—rose so high. He immediately offered Salieri the now vacant place of imperial royal chamber composer—which the appointee had been too modest to apply for—accompanied by a decree securing to him a salary of 100 ducats and free lodging. Joseph also appointed Salieri Kapellmeister to the Italian opera with a salary of 300 ducats—the now aged and feeble [Giuseppe] Bonno taking the place of Imperial Royal Court Kapellmeister.

Salieri's works this year (1774) were the comic opera with choruses, *La calamità de' cuori,* text by Goldoni—successful, and two cantatas of not great merit, for soli and chorus, composed for the benefit concerts of the Musicians' Widows and Orphans' Institute [*Witwen- und Waisen-Institut*].

In 1775 he set a comic opera by Gamerra, *La finta scema,* but the third act was feeble, and the work had little success.

⸭ ⸭ ⸭ ⸭ ⸭

The composer's love story comes in here and I agree with old Mosel that it is worth the reading. Not that it is much of a story, but one of those old men's reminiscences which carry the hearer or reader back with them into long past days—in which we rather like the innocent vanity running like a colored thread through the web, and which give us ofttimes (in the memoirs of old artists) such odd glimpses into their real characters, with their great want of religious principle, but superabundant religious faith in a providence specially provided for them. Now hear Salieri and see how lovingly he dwells upon that youthful love.

"In the course of this year I became acquainted with that angel whom God had appointed for my wife. In the year 1775, I gave music lessons to a young Countess who was receiving her education in the nunnery of St. Laurenz, and whom I had instructed before she went thither, at her father's house. In the same cloister other girls, mostly motherless, were boarded. My hour was from 11 to 12 a.m., and before it was finished these girls, accompanied by their guardians [dragons, duennas, *Aufseherinnen* —A.W.T.], usually passed through the music room to the dining hall. On the very first day of my lessons, one of these girls of slender figure, somewhat taller than the others, about eighteen years old and dressed in rose-colored taffeta, made a mighty impression upon me. Twice I saw her pass through the room, but the third and fourth time I sought her in vain among her companions, and knew not why she was absent which greatly troubled me. The fifth time the others came again without her; my restlessness increased, but she came later and alone following her companions. The unexpected joy which filled me, so mastered me that, as I bowed to her, of course with respect, it was in such a manner as to show her clearly that I had been pained not to see her the preceding days; and I believed I could see in her face just as plainly that it was not displeasing to her. From that moment her picture was firmly fixed in my head and heart; but the delicious feeling which accompanied the picture was modified by many a bitter thought. 'What folly,' I said to myself, 'to give way to such a sudden passion for a girl whom you have seen but three times, who has probably seen you for the first time here in the cloister, to whom you have never spoken, and probably never will speak! Moreover, who told you that she passed through the room the last time alone on your account? And suppose she has guessed the reason of your delight, are you certain that she shares in your feelings and has not already bestowed her inclinations upon some worthier object? But all such wise thoughts did not prevent my longing to see her again from increasing and on those days (days of torment for me!) when I had no call to the nunnery, I could not refrain from walking up and down under the windows of the room in which I supposed she was lodged.

"In this condition I lived when, on the second Sunday after my first meeting with the fascinating unknown, chance (or rather God's dispensation) gave me the opportunity to speak with her for the first time. I had been in the habit of attending, whenever I could, the Sunday afternoon service in the Cathedral. This time (it was in February) I came in rather late and found all the pews occupied; I placed myself therefore at the end of one where an old woman was kneeling who made a little space for me as well as she could. After finishing her devotions, the friendly old woman rose to go away; I stepped aside to let her pass and a young girl who had knelt beside her left the pew with her. Whom did I recognize in her? The young lady of the nunnery! What a heavenly surprise for me! I bowed to her with all respect, but without speaking; she, with much grace, returned the bow. It was impossible for me to remain one minute—I had to follow. I left the church, saw that she took the way to the nunnery with her companion, and hastened through other streets to get before her and to meet her. I wished to approach but dared not. At length, the fear of letting so good an opportunity slip roused my courage, and taking it for granted that she understood French, I besought her in that language to forgive my boldness and allow me to accompany her to the cloister. She answered me also in French, but with the voice and manner of an angel, that it would give her pleasure.

"I should attempt in vain to express the heartfelt delight with which these words and the perception that she was not displeased with the encounter filled me. With a voice trembling for very joy I continued the conversation; I prayed her to tell me her dear name. 'Therese von Helfersdorfer,' was the answer. I asked her how it came that I should have the happiness of meeting her at this hour (it was now about 6 p.m. and quite dark) out of the cloister, and why I had twice failed to see her pass through the music room? With amiable haste to satisfy my curiosity, she said that on those two occasions she had gone into the dining hall early, before my lesson hour, and that, since she had had the misfortune of losing her mother, she went every Sunday to visit her father and two younger brothers, and always returned to the nunnery at this hour accompanied by the old servant. Meantime, we had reached the cloister. I had not the courage to say more than that my habit was to attend service in the Cathedral every Sunday afternoon, and that if she allowed, I could always offer her my protection on the way back; to which with the same grace she answered that my company would give her pleasure, and added that she had already known my name even before she saw me in the cloister, and had often heard the young Countess (my pupil) speak of me in terms of praise. So now I understood why she at the first had met me in so friendly a manner. Intoxicated with joy at what I had heard, I wished her good night, and discussing with myself the singular meeting with her, I turned my steps—whither?—back into the Cathedral, to that spot where the beloved one had knelt, there to thank Heaven for its happy guidance, and to pray for continued blessings upon my honorable intentions; for a secret voice whispered to me that Therese was destined to make the happiness of my life.

"I longingly awaited the coming day to hurry to my lesson with the Countess in the cloister, but, just as I was on the point of leaving my room, a servant came to inform me that the Countess was ill, and I should not trouble myself again until further notice. What a thunderclap for me! All the joy of yesterday was suddenly banished; wrath in a thousand forms filled my breast, and, as during the whole week I was not called to my pupil, I may say I spent it in the jaws of purgatory. However, I embraced the opportunity of making inquiries in relation to the father of my beloved. He was an official, honored and respected, dwelling in his own house not far from St. Stephan's. It had hardly struck four o'clock the next Sunday, when I hurried to the church and placed myself near the door through which, coming from her father's house she had to enter. With strained attention, watching all who entered, how often I said to myself when someone resembled her at all: 'That is she—no!— now, at last—no, just as little as the other;' and this lasted three never-ending quarters of an hour. I was beginning to fear that she would not come at all, or that she had entered by another door; yes, still more painful doubts made me anxious; the Countess, it occurred to me, may not have been ill at all; the Abbess perhaps had charged her to keep me away after learning from Therese's servant ...; and so I martyred myself, until at last about five o'clock I saw the angel

and her companion enter. The prisoner condemned to death,
who unexpectedly sees his innocence proved, feels not such bliss
as streamed through me in that moment. After our devotions
were over I followed her as before, and found for all the pangs I
had endured sweet comfort in the assurance she gave me that it
gave her pleasure to see me again.

Non sa che sia diletto
Chi non provó nel petto
Un' innocente amor.
(Metastasio.)

"I asked my dear if the Countess really had been ill which she,
to the no small allaying of my recent doubts, answered in the
affirmative, adding that she would begin her lessons again the
next day. A thousand other thoughts crisscrossed through my
brain; I did not know where to begin, and the few moments at
my disposal were almost passed when I roused up courage to tell
her I had a secret to impart which concerned the peace of my
whole life, but besought her to promise me a decisive answer to
what I should say. She promised it and encouraged me with such
grace and with a sort of tender curiosity to speak, that I finally
had the boldness to say that I passionately loved her and wished
to learn if I could venture to hope for some, if but little, affection in return? 'For a like inclination,' she replied, half loud.
'For a like inclination!' I cried in transport as I seized her hand
and covered it with kisses. 'The same,' she repeated, lightly and
modestly pressing my hand. Beside myself for joy, I declared to
her that this assurance made me blessed, and asked when I
might present myself to her father in case she allowed me this
step. 'A week from today,' she said. 'I will prepare him for your
visit and you shall be well received, for my father already knows
you by reputation.' In fact, I had already at that time gained a
name through my successful operas, as *Armida, La fiera di Venezia,*
and *La secchia rapita,* and the gracious inclination of the Emper-
or toward me was also well known. However, it was not destined
that I should seek my beloved at the hands of her father; that
very week God suddenly called from this world the worthy old
gentleman, beloved by everybody, who had for some time been
ailing. At the same time the young Countess left Vienna for Hungary, and thus I was deprived of every opportunity of seeing

Therese, except now and then at the house of the parents of one of her companions.

"Herr von Helfersdorfer had appointed an excellent and rather wealthy man to be guardian of his daughter and two sons, who, a widower of middle age and ignorant of what had passed between his beautiful ward and me, had formed the plan of marrying her and soon after the father's death disclosed it to her. Of course there was nothing for Therese to do but declare the state of her feelings and the object of them. As soon as this came to my knowledge, I hastened to the guardian, accompanied by a man of high respectability, and made formal application for the hand of my charmer. He received me politely and declared with seeming equanimity, that since his ward was satisfied, he also consented to my demand; only he must be able to satisfy himself that I possessed sufficient means to support in respectability a wife who belonged to a family of rank and who possessed a not insignificant fortune. I replied that I earned 300 ducats as Kapellmeister of the Italian opera, a hundred ducats as imperial chamber composer, and had the hope of becoming Court Kapellmeister at some time; that, moreover, my compositions and music lessons brought me in another 300 ducats annually, so that I could well reckon my income at 700 ducats. The guardian answered: 'That would be more than sufficient if it were only certain; but, of all this, you can only rely upon the hundred ducats which you receive from Court; and I must therefore pray you to wait until your position improves in some positive manner before I, as guardian, can give my consent to this marriage.'

"Now in fact the honest man did no more than his duty—that I had to admit. I therefore only besought him to keep the matter for the present secret, which (to my good luck) he did *not* do.

"Two days afterward I went, as the duty of my office was, at 3 o'clock p.m. for the Emperor's chamber music gathering. When I entered the anteroom, I saw the monarch standing by the fireplace with his back toward me, alone and sunk in thought. He turned a little to see who came, and returned my respectful bow with his usual kindness. On the other side of the room stood the footman of the Emperor and two persons, one of whom, who had an appointment in the court library and was much liked by the Sovereign, was counted among my most intimate acquaintances. I joined them in silence, and my friend, smiling, made me the sign of the long nose.[1] At that moment the Emperor turned again, noticed the jest and came towards me asking what that meant. I pretended not to know, although in fact I understood the joke only too well! The librarian, however, in confusion stammered out that I had tried to marry a beautiful orphan, but had found a rival in her guardian. The monarch, at first somewhat surprised, but also smiling, asked me if this was true. I found myself now obliged to tell the whole history of my love, which seemed to amuse the Emperor much, and closed with the prayer that his majesty would forgive me for having kept the matter hitherto a secret; this I had done because the result was so uncertain. When I spoke of the reasons why the guardian refused his consent, I noticed a sudden but passing expression of seriousness; and when I finished, as he left me he said, as if half in thought to himself: 'Well then, you must have patience.' Meanwhile the other musicians had arrived and the concert began in its usual manner without a word more being said about my love affair.

"Next morning the Intendant of the Court music sent for me. I hastened to him and he greeted me with: 'Receive my congratulations, Herr Kapellmeister; the Emperor has raised your salary from one to three hundred ducats, with the single proviso that you shall lighten the burden of the excellent but now very old and often sick, Kapellmeister Bonno, and direct the Italian opera also, should his Majesty take it into his own hands.'[2] Most joyfully surprised, I thanked his Excellency for this unexpected communication, and was already on my way to Therese's guardian, when I thought of something better and turned my steps to the imperial palace. The monarch had hardly heard that I was in the anteroom, when he called for me. Sitting at his writing table, he called to me as I entered: 'Go,' the kindly prince interrupted me, 'Go to the guardian and this afternoon let me know his answer.'

"That I now flew to the guardian, that he could no longer refuse his consent, that the gracious monarch heard this with pleasure, and what thereupon followed, everyone can easily

[1] The same as the Masonic sign described in one of [Frederick] Marryatt's sea novels; and as my cousin Georgie's Japanese fan.—A.W.T.

[2] See *Ante*, that the Italian opera then was a private enterprise.—A.W.T.

imagine; but never will my grateful heart forget a goodness which gave me a happiness that I have now for many years enjoyed and now share with eight children who are the images of their beloved mother, and who even now sometimes listen again to the history of our loves with hearty enjoyment."

Does not that read like a chapter of Defoe?

♯ ♯ ♯ ♯ ♯

Though Joseph's taste was so decidedly for the Italian *opera buffa*, yet occasionally a serious opera was put upon the stage and sung by the *buffa* artists.[3] Giovanni di Gamerra had prepared a serious text, *Delmita e Daliso*, with choruses and dances, which, only after repeated entreaties, Salieri at last consented to compose. He had little hope that it would succeed; and though it was his only opera in the year 1776 and therefore not hastily written, his presentiment as to its fate was correct. And yet there were so many good things in it that Mosel is of the opinion that its fate was determined by the ridiculous accidents which occurred during the first performance.

The first scene is a rural amphitheater in which a crowd of peasants has assembled to see a wrestling match of shepherds. After the final rehearsal was over, the scene painter had the happy idea of painting into the turfy terraces and among the trees a great number of figures which added greatly to the scenic effect. After the games were over and the victors crowned, the crowd was to disperse leaving the head of the commune—whatever his title, Alcalde, Burgomaster, Mayor, first Selectman or 'Squire—with his two daughters alone. The great man has a secret to impart to them, and begins:

"Or che siam soli, o figlie." (Now we are alone, daughters.) As he recited these words and the audience saw the crowd of faces looking out from tree and bush, a laugh began which increased finally to a roar, as the singers looked in all directions in vain to make out the joke, since they were too near the scenery to make out the figures.

---

[3] I do not see why Holmes (*Mozart*, American edition, p. 50) should use this language in speaking of events in the winter of 1767-68: "There were no other singers at that time in Vienna; and will it be believed that with such a set they even atttempted Gluck's *Alceste!*" Shall a person of wit and humor never be serious? Should Gluck's *Alceste* go unsung because the singers so rarely performed in *opera seria*?—A.W.T.

In the second act Daliso, Delmita's lover, comes upon the stage armed, with the visor of his helmet down, to fight the monster to whom she is to be sacrificed by the laws of the land. As she flees in fright, he exclaims: "Non fuggir non temer, son' io Daliso" (Fly not, fear not, I am Daliso), and at the same moment has to raise the visor and show her his face. But "the fates, the sisters three and such odd branches of learning," were in a merry mood that evening and determined that the helmet should not open. So the more he tried to raise the visor, the tighter it seemed to be stuck and the louder the audience laughed. This was the joke of Act II.

After Daliso kills the monster the final scene shows Athens in the distance illuminated. The audience heard one of the singers recite: "Vedete come allo splendor di mille faci e mille festeggia Atene" (See how with the splendor of thousands and thousands of torches Athens rejoices)—but all was dark. The signal had been given too late to the workmen and not until the scene was ended and the curtain was descending did Athens blaze out amid the light of the "mille faci" and the uproarious laughter of the audience. In short, there seems to have been no such lamentable comedy and tragical mirth at Athens since the days of Quince, Snug and Bottom. Gamerra and Salieri's *opera seria* had proved an *opera buffa* and at the close the composer laughed as heartily as the audience.

The first attempt by Joseph to build up the German stage, and its failure, has been mentioned before; a new attempt under the influence of Sonnenfels, in 1770, had succeeded, and at the period to which we now arrive, 1776, the Court theater in Vienna surpassed all others in Germany in the excellence of its performances of German spoken dramas, as it had at one time surpassed the world in its Italian operas.

Fond as the Emperor was of his *opera buffa,* he now formed the magnanimous project of building up a real German opera. One management after another had broken down; the French company was dismissed; in 1774, Noverre, the ballet master, had to give place to the cheaper Angiolini; the receipts sank, and at the end of 1775, or early in 1776, the two court theaters came upon the hands of the Emperor. Hence, none of those "vested rights," which hinder progress in England in all directions, stood now in

Joseph's way. The Lower Austrian provincial government gave all the world notice that the Kärntnertor Theater was made free to any troupe which would undertake it at its own risk; and by an imperial order of February 17, 1776, the Burg Theater was given up to the Germans, and received the title *Hof- und National The- ater* (Court and National Theater).

Let a correspondent of the Leipzig *Allgemeine Musikalische Zeitung* (vol. 24, col. 253) add what is necessary to an understand- ing of the theatrical revolution headed by the Emperor of Ger- many, at the time the lawyer Adams, the printer Franklin, the merchant Hancock, the physician Warren, the farmer Putnam, the planter Washington, the shoemaker Sherman, and their compatriots and fellow lawyers, merchants, etc., were heading, across the water, a revolution of quite another sort.

"Joseph now had German drama performed four times a week; the prices were fixed at three gulden for the first and sec- ond boxes; first parterre one gulden; second parterre 20 Kreuzers; third row 30 Kreuzers and for the fourth row, 7 Kreuzers.[4] At first, the new stage—like everything which Joseph projected—found much opposition, but the daily presence and active sympathy of the Emperor by degrees filled the house; the success which was achieved was owing also, certainly in part, to the fact that all the German pieces were good and generally excellent. The permission to use the Kärntnertor house (which had been recently rebuilt, after catching fire at a performance of Gluck's ballet *Don Juan,* and burning down) was, after a failure or two by others, availed of by an Italian opera troupe, formed in part of the members of that which had just been dismissed. This troupe played at its own risk, was good and diligent, and there- fore soon gained the privilege of playing on the off days, also, in the Burg Theater. This company had seven men and six women solo singers, with Mlle. [Catarina] Cavalieri among the latter. In the Kärntnertor house, alternately with the Italian opera, Wäser's large troupe from Prussia tried its powers in the German drama and opera and in ballet, but the company was about equally bad in all three and soon fell to pieces.

[4] It is near enough the exact rate if we reckon the gulden at half a dollar, with 60 Kreuzers to the gulden; the new kreuzers are 100 to the gulden, 48 cents.—A.W.T., figuring 1864 dollars.

"As in everything else, so also in theatrical matters, it was the favorite idea of Joseph at that time—much as he personally enjoyed the Italian opera, to show himself a *German Emperor*—to favor in a special manner everything that was German—to have, as far as it was in any way possible, all in the German language and in German style.[5]

"This idea of Joseph's, his wide and varied knowledge, his great and quick activity, and his passion for the theater and music (for both, it is well known, he possessed uncommon talents, insight and skill) very soon effected much, which in one way and another proved of benefit and might have been more so, had his will been always so obeyed as it certainly ought to have been. For instance, in 1777, at his command and with his personal assistance, a plan was wrought out for the foundation of a school for the theater and for the establishment and selection of a dramatic library; and both, soon and to a certain extent, actually put into operation. It was advertised that every poet who contributed a piece which could be and really should be acted, should receive the entire proceeds of the third night as his due. Joseph soon after had a formal code of laws for the members of theatrical companies drawn up, which had been utterly wanting hitherto and for which the Parisian royal theatrical code served as a model.

"Towards the end of the year (1777) the Emperor at last made the experiment of founding an original German Opera for which the pieces should neither be translations nor adaptations of the music. He himself chose for the first trial a little work by Ignaz Umlauf [viola player in the orchestra]—which had only four vocal parts [rôles] and a chorus—called *Die Bergknappen*. The entire company [in its present infancy] consisted only of Mlle. Cavalieri, Madame Stierle, Herr [Martin] Ruprecht and Herr Fuchs—the two men having until now never trod the stage. Umlauf was made music director and Heinrich Müller, a man of fine taste and tact, manager. Joseph amused himself with the preparations and rehearsals, and the new and modest enter-

---

[5] If England could have had English kings after the revolution of 1688, with taste enough to encourage Purcell and his school, what might not have grown up out of the wonderful English, Scotch, Irish, and Welsh schools of melody—the most beautiful to my taste in the world!— A.W.T.

prise—which was at first made a topic of jest and ridicule, and which gave its first public performance on February 17, 1778[6]—gained great and soon general applause. Joseph thereupon increased the company with three new solo singers, two men and one woman, and the result was that during this year thirteen new pieces of greater or less extent were produced and the German opera established."

The "revolution" of course relieved Salieri from most if not all his operatic labors, at least for the time. After the failure of *Delmita e Daliso,* he composed an oratorio, *La passione di Gesù Christo,* text by Metastasio, for a performance by the Pension Institution of the Vienna Musicians [*Pensions-Institut der Wiener Tonkünstler*], which gained him great credit with the musically cultivated, and which, the poet once said in presence of the Emperor, was the most expressive music ever set to his poem. The overture was intended by the composer (*ipse dixit*) to express the repentance and despair of Peter, and is one of Salieri's best.

There is no account of any composition by Salieri in the year 1777; and after the success of Umlauf's operetta the Emperor, being full of the matter [in Spring 1778], gave his Kapellmeister leave to visit Italy, where his growing fame had now brought him three invitations to come and compose so many operas. In Milan a new opera house was to be opened—no less a one than the now famous La Scala—and all the old and well known composers of the Italian cities were passed over, to call their young countryman—now about twenty-seven years of age—from Vienna to write the opening piece. This was *Europa riconosciuta,* text by Verazi, in two acts, with choruses and an analogous ballet in the mid-

6 In Forkel's *Musikalische-Kritische Bibliothek,* Vol. II, 392, this first performance is thus reported:

Vienna, February 1778. Finally on the 17th inst., the first German operetta, *Die Bergknappen*—so impatiently expected—was produced. It surpassed the expectations of the public. The music and decorations were truly excellent. Mlle. Cavalieri, who formerly sang in the Italian opera buffa here, distinguished herself in singing several difficult and highly ornamented arias, and also by her much improved acting. Madam Stierle also received great applause. After the piece was ended and the curtain down, the audience demanded again the appearance of the performers. Thereupon all four came forward, and Mlle. Cavalieri delivered a very beautiful little speech of thanks to the spectators. His Majesty the Emperor is trying all means to bring these operettas into the mode and has the best subjects sought out. At present, all the solo parts are doubly filled so that there is no interruption caused by the indisposition of this or that singer. Our famous actor, Herr Müller, has the duty of instructing in action; Herr Umlauf in singing, etc., etc.—A.W.T.

dle of each act. Premiered on August 3, 1778, the piece had
great success in spite of a miserable text, and long kept its place
on the stage, though Mosel thinks it one of Salieri's poorer compositions.

From Milan the composer went to Venice to compose *La scuola de' gelosi*, an opera buffa, text by Mazzolà, which was brought
out early in 1779 [actually December 27, 1778] and had extraordinary success. Salieri had with him on this tour a young German, now for the first time in Italy, who lodged with him in
Venice and accompanied him everywhere. The day succeeding
the opening of the theaters after Christmas is, or rather was
(while the state of Venice existed), a day for the assembling of all
who cared for music and the drama, in the coffeehouses about
the Piazza San Marco, to discuss or inquire about the new pieces
with which the various houses had opened. It is the custom in
that city to name the theaters from the nearest church, but in
talking about them to call them by the name of the saint only—
instead, for instance, of saying "the theater near the church of St.
Samuel," or "Teatro Sant' Angiolo," to merely say "San Samuele,"
or "Sant' Angiolo." On this morning Salieri with his companion
took his coffee in one of the largest houses on the square, where
the theatrical news was of course the main topic of conversation.

"Saint Benedict was hissed off," said one. "The Angel was pretty successful, but Saint Samuel went to the devil," said another,
and so on. On leaving the house, the young German, astounded
and indignant, remarked to Salieri: "How disrespectfully they do
talk here of the saints!"

From Venice the composer journeyed to Rome to compose the
opera buffa, *La partenza inaspettata*, text by Petrosellini, which,
with its beautiful, flowing melodies, corresponding exquisitely to
the text, and its fine but simple accompaniment, in some of the
vocal pieces consisting only of the quartet of bowed instruments,
was another complete triumph [actually premiered December
22, 1779].

These successes led to offers of new engagements which, with
Joseph's permission, Salieri accepted, and therefore in the
spring of 1779, he returned to Milan to compose *Il talismano*,
text by Goldoni, for the opening of another new theater—Alla
Cannobiana [August 21, 1779]. This was also an opera buffa with

choruses, in two acts.

Passing through Florence on his way north, he found the manager of the principal house just ready to bring out his *La fiera di Venezia,* and that functionary besought him to at least be present at the general rehearsal to which he consented. The rehearsal was set for the evening. The hour had struck, and the soloists and orchestra were ready, but not a chorus singer was to be seen. "Why are they so late?" asked Salieri. "Because the shops are not shut," was the answer. The explanation for this was that most of the Italian choruses then were made up of shopkeepers or their assistants who, not knowing one note from another, learned their parts by rote and never made a mistake—but they had only Italian choruses to sing.

The directors of the new Cannobiana theater, three noblemen of Milan, had arranged to open the house with three works: Salieri's *Fiera di Venezia, Il talismano,* and finally, an opera to be set by a composer named Russ [actually Giacomo Rust, 1741-1784]. While the vocalists were studying the first, Salieri set himself to work upon the second, of which Goldoni had sent from Paris the first act and the plan of the whole. The second act was delayed by the sickness of Goldoni. Then the theater was not ready in time, and, as the singers were only engaged up to a certain date, it became impossible to produce the third of the proposed operas, and poor Russ saw himself deprived of the opportunity of proving his talents and of necessity had to content himself with a present made by the directors and a written invitation for an engagement during the next season. Salieri pitied the man in his bitter disappointment, and, satisfied with having one of his operas performed, he proposed to the directors that they give the second act of *Il talismano* which had now arrived, to Russ. They did this; Russ composed it, and the work was a complete success.

A change in the management of the theater in Venice, the old manager having died, and the want of sufficient security that his time and labor would be adequately rewarded, led Salieri to give up the composition of *L' isola capricciosa,* which the poet Mazzolà had already sent him and of which he had already several numbers finished. He therefore remained some time longer in Milan and then returned to Rome to compose another opera text by

Petrosellini, *La dama pastorella,* for the Carneval of 1780, a work
which he himself says "neither pleased nor displeased."

In Rome he received an invitation to Naples where Joseph's
disreputable sister Caroline was queen, to compose a serious
opera for San Carlo, to be brought out in May 1780, and to prepare his *Scuola de' gelosi* for production upon the so-called Floren-
tine Theater. A third leave of absence was therefore necessary.
The composer was long in doubt whether he could with propri-
ety apply again for an extension of his leave; but as it was for only
three months, and as he had received the invitation through the
Austrian Ambassador, Count von Lamberg, and with the appro-
bation of the King of Naples—Joseph's brother-in-law—he took
courage and sent on his application to Count [Franz Xaver Wolf]
Orsini-Rosenberg (1723-1796), chief chamberlain and head of
the court theater at Vienna—him, who had the previous year
obtained the prolongation of his leave of absence—and went on
to Naples to begin his work and await the reply. His petition was
written in the most respectful terms, and his reasons displayed in
the clearest light, and there is no doubt that, had Joseph read it,
the three months would have been granted him at once. But
Rosenberg, as he afterwards confessed, placed the petition in his
cabinet and forgot it, and made Salieri's desire known to Joseph
in few words and with no explanation of the circumstances
under which the petition was written and which certainly justified it. The result was that the composer received the following
answer:

> "In reply to the petition addressed to his Majesty for
> leave to remain still longer in Italy, his Supreme High-
> ness makes it my duty to write you, saying that you are
> your own master to remain there as long as you please
> or think for your good; indeed, that if you find yourself
> better off there than here, you may remain there forev-
> er. I am pained to be unable to make you any pleasan-
> ter reply and remain, etc., etc."

It was a very unlucky mistake of Salieri's not to have sent word
to Rosenberg with his petition that, in the hope of receiving the
desired leave, he was going on to Naples in order to save all the
time possible. The ungracious reply was sent to Rome and from
there forwarded by a friend to him in Naples. Meanwhile Salieri

had waited upon Count Lamberg and had been presented at court, where the king and queen had received him with great favor. He had also begun the composition of his opera, *La Semiramide.*

The surprise and fright with which Rosenberg's letter filled him were overwhelming. Lamberg, to whom Salieri hastened to ask his advice, sought to calm him by persuading him that if the queen should apply to her brother on his behalf the matter would have no serious consequences. Salieri therefore determined to apply at once to the queen, but as he returned to his lodgings and thought it over, he saw the matter in a very different light. He remembered that Joseph, who invariably was friendly towards every man and especially to those constantly about him, did not like to be forced to say yes where he had once said no. Filled with anxiety lest the mere refusal of his petition might not be all, but that a loss of his master's favor might follow, he returned to Count Lamberg and, most urgently entreating him to find a way of cancelling his engagement with the Neapolitan court, departed on the instant for Vienna. Before entering his carriage he wrote to Count Rosenberg entreating forgiveness for his too great freedom, and announcing his immediate departure from Naples.

At noon on April 8, 1780, he rejoined his delighted family—that is on the second anniversary of the day on which he began his Italian journey. His first call was upon Rosenberg; but not finding him at home, he went to the palace and, as a mark of his submission to the will of the Emperor, instead of proceeding into Joseph's apartment as his right was and as he had always done, remained outside in the corridor where petitioners awaited their monarch, who came there every afternoon at three o'clock to hear them and receive their papers. There, a little apart from some twenty persons, mostly country people, who awaited the Emperor, Salieri took his place not a little afraid of a cool reception.

At the usual hour, Joseph returned from a ride, came as usual through the corridor, listened to the petitioners, talked with them more like a father than a monarch, and suddenly caught sight of the Kapellmeister. Hastening to him he exclaimed:

"See, here is Salieri! I did not expect you so soon; have you had a pleasant journey?"

"An excellent one, your majesty," he answered timidly, "notwithstanding, in order to correct my error for which I humbly pray forgiveness, I felt bound to travel day and night that I might so much the sooner resume my duties here at court."

"It was not necessary to hurry so," said Joseph, kindly, "still it is a pleasure for me to see you again. Now go upstairs, we will try some pieces out of your new operas which have been sent to me from Italy."

These good words so calmed and encouraged the musician that he forgot all the troubles which his hurried journey had caused him. On entering the antechamber he found some of the older members of the Court Chapel [*Hofkapelle*], who rejoiced all the more to see him since a report had obtained currency that he had fallen under the Emperor's displeasure. Half an hour later came Joseph who put the petitions and documents which he had received into his cabinet, seated himself to his dinner in the music room, and had Salieri called in to talk with him during his solitary meal of fifteen minutes duration. "Had he found his family all well?" he asked, and put various questions in relation to his tour, to his compositions while away, and the like. Salieri told his story, and of course, came at last to the Neapolitan business. As in some confusion, he confessed that he had left Rome for Naples without waiting for permission to do so, in full faith that this permission would follow him, Joseph, with a sudden turn of his head—one of his peculiarities—fixed his eyes upon him with an expression of surprise. Salieri ceased and there was a moment's pause during which he (Salieri) thought his master, who had not known that the matter had gone so far, was sorry not to have granted his petition. Still he said nothing and gave the conversation a new turn by the question: "Where did you find the best orchestra?" Salieri saw that nothing more was to be said on the Naples affair and bore himself accordingly.

After his meal the other musicians were called in and Joseph devoted his usual concert hour to pieces from *Europa riconosciuta,* and *La scuola de' gelosi*. The concert over, Salieri was told to visit in the evening the new *"National Singspiel"* (Singing-drama), as Joseph called his German opera. "You must then tell me," added the Emperor, "if the company and the establishment have made progress during your absence." At the next private concert, Joseph asked as soon as he saw Salieri. "How do you find our *National Singspiel?*" The composer, really pleased with what he had seen and heard, replied that he had found it in all respects wonderfully perfect. "Now you shall compose a German opera," said Joseph. Salieri proposed the translation of one of his fine operas composed in Italy. "No translation," returned the other, smiling, "an original *Singspiel!*"

"Your majesty, I do not know how to set about the work of an opera in the German language, I speak it so badly." "Well, then," said Joseph, still smiling, "the labor will serve as an exercise in the language. Tomorrow morning I will give Count Rosenberg the order to have a German operatic poem prepared for you."

This, which was proposed in a light-hearted manner, Salieri had to carry out in full earnest—for which, however, he had plenty of leisure, as Maria Theresa happened to die soon after (November 29, 1780), and the court theaters were of course closed for some weeks.

CHAPTER 5

Singspiel, Paris and Da Ponte

THE NEXT YEAR (1781) appeared from Salieri's pen a ballad opera in German, entitled *Der Rauchfangkehrer* (Chimney-sweeper). The author of the text was unknown to Mosel since it was one which a friend [Theodor Auenbrugger] had given to Salieri so that he might practice setting German words to music while waiting for a text from the directors of the theater. Still, it was put upon the stage and, in spite of the critics, was a success not only in Vienna but in other cities—for instance, Bonn where the boy Ludwig van Beethoven had the opportunity of hearing it. Mosel says that the sharp criticisms of the work can only have related to the text, which, he adds, was beneath criticism both in its style and versification while the music deserves special commendation. Salieri's success in setting what to him was still a strange language, he says, was surprising and the modulations in the music—the entire accompaniments—were very beautiful. As a joke, a burlesque, in a tenor aria of this work, Salieri introduced a passage which was sung in falsetto, since nobody in those days dreamed that that thin, expressionless, unmanly kind of tone could ever come to be employed by composers except to create a laugh.

Leopold Mozart, in 1783, wrote to his son in Vienna for a copy of this work for Salzburg, and on December 10, received the following reply[1]: "I only write you in greatest haste that I have bought *Der Rauchfangkehrer* for six ducats and have it already at home. Judging from your letter you take it to be an Italian opera. No, it is in German and, moreover, a miserable original piece

---

[1] Emily Anderson, ed., *The Letters of Mozart and His Family,* third edition (New York: W.W. Norton, 1985), No. 501.—T.A.

which has Dr. Auenbrugger, here in Vienna, for its author. You will remember that I told you about Herr Fischer's having publicly satirized it on the stage."

In 1782, Salieri received an order to compose an opera seria for the court stage in Munich. He gladly undertook this, the more so because he was allowed to take Metastasio's *Semiramide* for his text, of which he had composed several numbers in Naples. This also proved to be a success.

The next year, Joseph having re-established his Italian opera with a company selected from a list of singers made by Salieri in Italy, the season opened with Salieri's *La scuola de' gelosi,* enriched with several new numbers, which was a new triumph for the composer.

It will be remembered that one of the persons, who in 1770 tried over Salieri's youthful production *Le donne letterate* and encouraged its production, was Gluck. The accumulating evidence of the young man's talents, his lively disposition, and especially his taste and views in music and composition, had won the warm affection of the veteran composer and his fullest confidence. Of this he now gave a striking proof. At the end of 1783, since Gluck was no longer able to undertake an opera in consequence of a previous stroke of apoplexy, he was called upon by the directors of the French Academy of Music to designate some other composer, able to produce a French opera on the principles of that philosophy in Art, which he had taught both by precept and example, and which alone could give birth to truly dramatic music. Gluck proposed Salieri, now in his thirty-third year.

It was twenty years since the first performance of *Orfeo ed Euridice* in Vienna (1764) [*sic*]. *Alceste* and *Paride ed Elena* (*Paris and Helen*) followed in course of time and, having gained that success which makes them mark an era in operatic history, the contest between his and the old Italian and French styles was renewed in the French language at Paris. "At last," says Poisot, "on April 19, 1774, *Iphigénie en Aulide* of Chevalier Gluck made its first appearance in the Nouvelle Salle du Palais Royal, which had been opened on January 26, 1770, by a reproduction of Rameau's *Zoroastre.*"

Here is the list of Gluck's operas in Paris:
  1774, April 19. *Iphigénie en Aulide.* 3 Acts. Text by Racine,

arranged for the opera by du Roullet.

1774, August 2. *Orphée et Eurydice*. 3 Acts. Text by Calzabigi, translated and adapted in French by
Moline.

1776, April 23. *Alceste*. 3 Acts. Text by Calzabigi, translated by du Roullet.

1777, September 23. *Armide*. 5 Acts. Text by Quinault.

1779, May 18. *Iphigénie en Tauride*. 4 Acts. Text by Guillard.

1779, September 24. *Écho et Narcisse*. 3 Acts. Text by de
Tschudi.

The order now received from Paris was for an opera in the
style of these, and the text selected was *Les Danaïdes,* by François
Louis du Roullet and Ludwig Theodor von Tschudi. Gluck's recommendation was of course sufficient and the composition was
entrusted to Salieri. It was his first attempt to compose a French
text, his first attempt also to leave the regular Italian forms,
which alone his protector Joseph really found to his taste. Salieri
himself honestly recorded the fact that he composed the work
under the guidance of Gluck. (See Appendix B.) When it was
finished he took it to Gluck and they went through it together at
the pianoforte. In one of the arias was a passage with which the
composer was dissatisfied but was unable to find where the fault
consisted. He pointed it out in the score to Gluck who examined
it and then called upon Salieri to sing it. He listened attentively
and then said: "You are right, dear friend, the aria as a whole is
good, but the passage with which you are dissatisfied displeases
me also. Still I cannot at the moment discover the reason. Sing
the aria again." Salieri did so. "And now again." When the other
reached the passage now for the third time Gluck interrupted
him and suddenly exclaimed: "Now I have it—the passage smells
of music!" and upon examination they found that the musical
idea here did not spring from any necessity of the situation or
sentiment in the text, but was introduced simply on artistic
grounds.

"This remark of the great man," said Salieri, "is as original as it
is full of meaning, and in the highest degree instructive for every
artist in every art."

Salieri himself took his score to Paris, not only with the consent, but to the great pleasure of Joseph. *Les Danaïdes* was put upon the stage with immense splendor and first publicly performed on April 26, 1784, in the *Theatre de la Porte St. Martin,* the Palais Royal theater having been burned a few years before. The success of the work was such as to gain him an order for two new operas. Rauquit-Lieutaud wrote him that every composer who produced three successful works at the Academy received for each of the first twenty performances 200 francs, for each of the ten following 150 francs, for each of the next (the fourth) ten 100 francs, and all beyond forty 60 francs.

Cramer, in his *Magazin der Musik* (II, 417 *et seq.*), gives a long article made up out of various numbers of the *Mercure de France* upon *Les Danaïdes.* The article, of course, with its account of Danaus, Hypermnestra, the children of Danaus, of Linceus and his brethren, and the story of the five act drama, I pass over; but the introductory notice by Cramer himself is of too much interest to leave untranslated. Here it is:

"If the German public, and especially those who have formed a better acquaintance with Salieri through the pianoforte arrangement of *Armida* which I have published, are as curious as I am to learn something of his new work since, to all appearance, he has followed in it still more closely the footsteps of Gluck and the path of Nature, they will thank me for giving them here a detailed and very intelligent criticism of it, both text and music, drawn from the *Mercure de France,* a work far too little known in Germany. True, I should have much preferred to have first seen the score of the opera, which as I hear with great satisfaction is soon to appear in Paris, in order to add to the news which these articles give my own more detailed opinion of it; but it may well be some time before we shall receive the score. Still I will introduce some notes of my own which, perhaps, the thoughtful critic may not look upon as quite superfluous.

"I knew long ago, through letters received before Salieri left Vienna for Paris, that at first *Les Danaïdes* was to pass in Paris under the name of Gluck, to save it from the ill-natured remarks which so many who judge a work of genius by the name of its author and not after its own merits would be ready to make, as well as to smooth its way to the stage. Very soon after his arrival in Paris, I received from Vienna the following account of its success. '*Les Danaïdes* thus far is having all possible luck. People have again come upon the idea that the entire opera is by Gluck and thus the composer is saved from a thousand plagues and torments in bringing it out, which would be far from the case in respect to a new master making his first appearance. The queen has had him come to Versailles three times to rehearse the work there; and each time has herself sung with the *professori*. Salieri is to conduct once more there in presence of the king, Count d' Artois and several high personages of the court of both sexes. He will have cause for full satisfaction if the piece finds the same success with the public in Paris that it has enjoyed at court.'

"In another letter, which he himself wrote to the secretary of the chamber of finance in Vienna, Herr Josef von Paradies, father of the famous blind *pianiste* Maria Theresia von Paradies, he said among other things: 'Ritter Gluck spoke but the truth when he asserted that if the composer demands twenty livres for writing an opera, he ought to have twenty thousand for the trouble in bringing it out.'

"Finally, after his return from Paris, Salieri wrote me in relation to the success of his work, with all the noble modesty and frank ingenuousness which give such increased value to his talents, as follows:

Vienna, July 20, 1784.

"… And so I am at length back again from Paris. As to the news in relation to *Les Danaïdes,* which you ask of me, I could do nothing more than repeat what you have no doubt already read in the *Journal de Paris* and the *Mercure de France.* In the former you have doubtless noted the indecision of the Parisian public as to the value or want of it of the work, and the praise together with the censure in detail (in No. 21), as well as in the latter, the declaration, as to the real author of the music of Ritter Gluck. I have not yet heard what people think of the opera since. During my stay there it was given thirteen times.

"I only succeeded on the first two evenings in hearing the performance well and then through special favor; the other times I had no desire to go early and wait two hours to secure a good place and hence could neither

see nor hear well. Some people have said all this is
good, others all that is bad of it: some would have it that
the music was mine; others not; and this in spite of the
public declaration of Ritter Gluck and my reply to it.
What was there further to be done?

"The direction of the Paris opera have, since that declaration of Ritter Gluck, ordered the composition by
me of two new dramatic poems: the one entitled *Axur
(Tarare) King of Ormus,* the other *Les Horaces et Curiaces.*[2]
This last will probably be the one which I shall first
complete. This is the advice of Gluck; and the other
requires too much time on account of the peculiar
manner in which the subject is treated. The public as a
rule enjoys and seeks the truth in music; I therefore,
who without this truth should hate the art, feel myself
inclined, in the highest degree inclined, to exert all my
powers, to make myself worthy its applause, and therefore hope and believe that I shall hardly be forced to
write Italian operas again.

"The 'declaration of Ritter Gluck' here mentioned was a letter
printed in the *Journal de Paris,* in which the veteran declared the
music of *Les Danaïdes* to be wholly by Salieri, and that he himself
had no share in its production beyond the advice which he had
given the composer."

In the meantime Salieri's *Armida* (composed in 1771) was
making its way throughout Germany and even beyond. In
Copenhagen it was given in Italian and Danish, and C.F. Cramer,
the editor of the Musical Magazine at Altona, had prepared a
German version with which it was given at Bonn, Mainz and
Frankfurt am Main. A letter of Cramer to Salieri is valuable for
its clear enunciation of the duty of a translator in preparing ver-
sions of texts to musical compositions.

"I venture to affirm," says he, "that it is less difficult for a
poet—supposing him to have some creative talent—to compose
three original operatic poems, than to translate one to an opera
already set to music. There are arias in *Armida* which have cost
me weeks; arias which day and night I have had to turn over in

---

[2] In Salieri's Italian original, these are cited as *Atar, Re d'Ormus* and *gli Orazi e li Curi-
azi.*—T.A.

mind a thousand times in order at last to find the right word, the suitable syllable, the proper vowel sound, which this or that passage of the melody demands. Still I do not flatter myself to have achieved a perfect success, which is all the more difficult because of the various inflections and repetitions of a music which in the highest degree is exact and characteristic in its expression, and from the character of my native language, which, though strong, expressive and better suited than yours to reflect the most difficult versifications and rhythms of the Greek, is still at times not agreeable to the ear, nay even rough and in this regard stands far beneath the tongue of Hesperia [i.e., Italy] which Melody herself would seem to have created expressly for music."

In the preface to Kunzen's pianoforte arrangement [1783] of *Armida* with the above named German text, Cramer says of Salieri:

"Following in the footsteps of Gluck, the conqueror of hearts, he has like him turned away from the old conventional paths; treating with contempt the old useless *ritornels* and *da capos,* the sing-song of expressionless passages, the glitter of mere musical effects which only destroy the illusion of the scene, he has introduced more fitting proportions in his arias, a judicious shortening of the numerous choruses, not seldom more labor than is common in his recitative, the most imposing picturesqueness in his overtures, and great variety in his instrumentation; song and the dance are joined; everything is calculated for the general effect and he has succeeded everywhere in expressing the passions of the text with such heart-felt, melting, soul-touching song, that the entire opera from beginning to end seems to be nothing but such a *pezzo di prima intenzione,* as it rejoices one to find even one or two examples of it in the works of the better masters; while beyond that there is opportunity enough, in the rest of the arias, for the hearer to cool the fire kindled in his heart." It is quite inconceivable, adds Mosel, that a man who could so appreciate this work and could so well translate the text, should introduce three arias of other composers (Leo, Hasse and Sacchini) instead of certain recitatives which seemed to him too long—at which Salieri, justly, was very angry.

Armida not only delighted the public wherever it was put upon the stage, but found no dissenting voice among the critics.

Johann Adolph Scheibe, a learned musician and thoroughly grounded in the theory, a valued writer on the science, a man whom Sebastian Bach called doctor and teacher[3], heard it in Copenhagen and blessed the good fortune "which had caused him in his old age to hear an opera that embodied his ideas of what an opera should be, since it banished all the conventional ornamentation and depended for its success alone upon nature and the heart."

Soon after Salieri's return to Vienna, Pierre Louis Moline, Parliamentary Advocate in Paris, wrote him that his opera-text *La foire de Venise,* a French version of Salieri's *Fiera di Venezia,* had been read in the committee of the Royal Academy and had greatly pleased; he therefore asked the master to finish what remained to be done in the adaptation as soon as possible, and this the more urgently because Marie Antoinette wished to have the "Comedie-Ballet," as Moline now called it in its new form, produced at Fontainebleau. A few months later Moline wrote to Gluck to have him hasten Salieri with his work, but it does not appear that the work was brought out in Paris. Almost simultaneously came a letter from Rauquit-Lieutaud informing him that the changes in his new text, *Mahomet II,* which the Committee of the Academy had demanded, had been made, that the work was accepted and he only awaited a hint from Salieri to send it at once to him for composition. True, nothing came of this, but these letters indicate the position which *Les Danaïdes* had given the composer in Paris.

When Lorenzo da Ponte came from Dresden to Vienna in 1782 or 1783 [actually 1781]—the old fellow is very sparing of dates in his memoirs—he brought the following note of introduction:

> Friend Salieri: My dearest friend! Da Ponte will bring you these few lines. Do everything for him that you would do for myself. His heart and his talents deserve it all, and besides this he is *Pars animae, dimidiumque meae.*
>
> Yours, Mazzolà

"Salieri was at that time," says old Lorenzo (writing some forty years afterwards [1823-1827] in New York), "a favorite of the Emperor, the most intimate friend of Mazzolà, very learned and accomplished both as Kapellmeister and as a man of high consid-

---

[3] Mosel and Thayer partially confuse J.A. Scheibe with his father, Johann.—T.A.

eration among scholars. This billet, which I did not neglect to deliver immediately upon my arrival in Vienna, in process of time brought me the noblest fruits and was the original cause of the favor bestowed upon me by Joseph II." Omitting Da Ponte's account of his poverty for the months that followed we come to his tale of Salieri's kindness to him.

"I happened to learn that the Emperor had determined again to establish an Italian opera in Vienna and this recalled to mind the hints I had had from Mazzolà, and so the idea entered my head of becoming poet at the court of the Emperor.[4] I had always cherished for this ruler a feeling of the truest reverence because numberless proofs of humanity, magnanimity, and goodness of heart were told about him. This feeling gave me courage and strengthened my hopes. I went to Salieri, who not only encouraged me to apply for the position, but also promised me to speak not only with the general director of the theater, but with the Emperor himself on the subject. He knew so well how to move in the matter that my first appearance before the Emperor was not to petition, but to thank him for the appointment."

Il ricco d'un giorno (The Rich Man for a Day) was Da Ponte's first text written for Salieri by whom the subject had been selected out of many which the young poet had proposed. When finished, however, it was so far from reaching his ideal that he handed it to the composer too much humbled to speak a word. Salieri read it through immediately and then said: "It is well written, but it must first be seen on the stage before one can form a correct judgment upon it. It contains several very good arias and entire scenes which please me much; still, you will have to undertake some small changes for me, more however on the ground of the musical effect than anything else."

"Wherein consisted these light changes?" asked Da Ponte. "In the shortening or lengthening the greater part of the scenes; in the introduction of new duets, trios, quartets, etc.; in changing the metre of some half of the arias; in weaving in choruses which had to be sung by Germans; in shortening all the recitatives and, consequently, changing the entire plan, connection, and interest of the opera—if it had had any. In a word, the changes were so great that when the opera came upon the stage, not more than a

[4] Metastasio had died on April 12, 1782.—A.W.T.

hundred verses of my original remained." The music was finished and the work was to be soon performed when Abbate
[Giambattista] Casti (1724-1803), an ecclesiastical poet then celebrated through all Europe not only for his other poems but for
his *Galante Novellen,* tales in verse of a character immoral almost
to obscenity, appeared. At the same time came [Giovanni]
Paisiello, the composer, and the *Rich Man for a Day* was put aside
for *King Theodore of Venice* [*Il re Teodoro in Venezia*], text by Casti,
music by Paisiello. This opera had an enormous success and
soon found its way, in Italian and German, all through central
Europe—it was one of the favorite operas in Bonn when
Beethoven was a youth.

All this had happened in 1783, and Salieri, wisely giving *King
Theodore* time to become an old story, laid his *Rich Man* aside and
went off to Paris with his *Danaïdes,* as before related. In the
Autumn of 1784 the *Rich Man* was produced. It was unsuccessful—Mosel thinks undeservedly so—and Da Ponte gives a long
and not uninteresting history of the reasons of its fall. Among
them was the illness of Nancy Storace, the London songstress,
who at that time was a favorite prima donna in Vienna and whose
part had to be sung by a person "who was just as fitted for it as a
dove to take the rôle of an eagle." And what was worse, some Italians who wished for the place to which Da Ponte had just been
appointed, wrote a satire upon the libretto and circulated it in
the theater on the evening of its production. Nothing saved the
young poet but Joseph's liking of him and justice in determining
that he should have another trial. This second trial was the *Il
burbero di buon cuore* set to music by [Vicente] Martín [y Soler],
(the Spaniard, afterwards composer of *Una cosa rara*) and the
success was such that Joseph said to Da Ponte: "*We* have conquered!" And again, when Da Ponte called at the palace, the
Emperor received him with "Bravo, Da Ponte, it pleases me, both
music and text." "Sacred Majesty," replied the poet, "the Director
of the theater is quite of another opinion." "Neither the Director
nor Casti is speaking now," returned Joseph, "but this is your triumph, you have made them weep. Go home, get up courage,
and write us another opera with music by Martín. One must weld
the iron while it is hot."

After the production of *Eraclito e Democrito,* operetta in two acts, of which I find no account,[5] Salieri turned to Abbate Casti for a text and received *La grotta di Trifonio,* which he composed in 1785. "This music," said Salieri, "in a style as unusual as the poem demands, gained remarkable applause and was the first opera buffa to be engraved in score." Mosel remarks:

> This is all that the modest composer says of a work which has its place not only among his very best, but among the very best of its class, and deserves the title of classic; it is but right to add that none could remember any opera up to that time which had been received with such tumultuous, universal and lasting applause as this, and that all lovers of dramatic music still (1826) remember with delight the enjoyment it then afforded them. The most judicious and flowing melodies, invariably suited in perfection to the text and character represented; an expressive and graceful accompaniment, in which the wind instruments are more frequently (but not too often) and elegantly introduced than in any of his previous operas; and that talent, already noted in several of these works, for making his music really dramatic, through its vivid support, often indeed its actual indication, of the proper action, placed this work in the high position of a lasting model of high-comic, scenic music.

The date of the first performance of this work, which soon found its way in the Italian or in German translation into all the principal theaters of Germany, was May 12,[6] 1785.

On the 7th of February, 1786, Joseph gave an entertainment for Catherine II of Russia and her son Paul at Schönbrunn, at which two short occasional pieces, one in German, *Der Schauspieldirektor* (The Theatrical Manager) by Stephanie the younger, and *Prima la Musica, poi le parole,* (First the Music, Then the Text) by Abbate Casti, were performed. In the composition of the music, Mozart and Salieri were pitted against each other. Neither, however, produced anything of great value. Mozart's music is, however, with another text, still given [1864] in Germany;

[5] Angermüller lists its premiere as Vienna, August 13, 1795.—T.A.
[6] Angermüller lists October 12.—T.A.

Salieri's has long since been forgotten. The performances of the festivity were repeated (Salieri's operetta in German translation?) in the Kärntnertor Theater on February 11, 18, and 25 [1786], and then both were laid aside until 1791, when Goethe caused Cimarosa's *L'impresario in angostie* to be prepared for performance at Weimar, and in this the entire music of Mozart's *Manager* was incorporated! This was given on October 24, 1791, and from there made its way to other theaters. Recently [ca. 1863] Mozart's music has been taken again, pure and simple and, a few of his own compositions being added, a score extensive enough has been created to fit a new text in which Schikaneder and Mozart himself are made to appear—Mozart abominably caricatured! But this is foreign to Salieri's life.

CHAPTER 6

Mozart

T HE RELATIONS WHICH EXISTED between Mozart and Salieri have been a fruitful topic for three-fourths of a century. As we have now reached the period of the composition of *The Marriage of Figaro*, this is the proper place to deal with a by no means easy subject. Holmes' remark that *Figaro* was undertaken at the suggestion of Emperor Joseph is a mistake.[1] Da Ponte, finding it necessary to write something which should justify Joseph in retaining him as Court Poet and conquer Abbate Casti and his party and knowing but two composers whom he, at the time, was willing to write for, set himself, as he says, "earnestly at work to think out a pair of dramas for my dear friends, Mozart and Martín ... As to the first, I saw easily that his boundless genius demanded a broad, many-sided and noble subject. As I talked with him one day on this topic, he asked me whether I could, without too much trouble, form a text out of the comedy of Beaumarchais, entitled *The Marriage of Figaro*."

Thus the idea was originated by Mozart himself and this was in the Autumn of 1785; for, on November 2, he wrote to his father and excused the shortness of the letter on the ground that he was excessively occupied with *Le Nozze di Figaro*. Da Ponte asserts positively that the opera, text and music, was finished in six weeks. This may be so, for Mozart's entry in his own catalogue—(1786) "29 April, *Le Nozze di Figaro*"—may refer to the completion of the Overture which, of course, had not been needed until the work came to rehearsal—and the first stage rehearsal had taken place the day before (April 28)—and thus Holmes is again corrected, who believed that the work was

---

[1] See Holmes, *Life of Mozart*, American edition, p. 199.—A.W.T.

entirely written in that month of April!

Again, Holmes says: "Salieri and Righini, being at this time ready with operas, were both competitors with Mozart for preference."[2] His authority is, of course, Kelly, who says that three operas were now ready: *Il Demogorgone* by Righini, *Figaro,* and *La grotta di Trophonio* by Salieri. But we have already seen that Salieri's opera was given on October 12 of the preceding year and we shall see, when the thread of the narrative is again resumed, that he was at this time too busy with his two operas for Paris to have any time or inclination to stand in the way of Mozart. We shall see, moreover, that he left Vienna in the spring of 1786 and did not return until October, 1787. When Mozart's father, therefore, writes to his daughter in April, 1786: "Salieri and all his tribe will move heaven and earth to put it (*Figaro*) down," whatever may have been the Italian's desire in the premises he was not in Vienna at the critical time; nor could he have been the cause that after Martín's *Cosa rara* came upon the stage, on November 17, 1786, Mozart's work was laid aside. The fact is that Joseph's taste was not cultivated up to Mozart's magnificent instrumentation. From what we have already seen of him and his taste in music, how could it be?

One more passage from Holmes is worth quoting to show the danger of trusting the fancy in writing history: "Few have been the instances in dramatic annals in which men of such renown as Haydn, Mozart, Gluck, Paisiello, Storace, Salieri, Righini, Anfossi, etc., have been collected under one roof to witness the first performance of an opera, as it is no improbable surmise that they were on this occasion," viz: the production of *Figaro* on the first evening of May, 1786. The "surmise" is, on the other hand, very improbable. The strong probability is that Haydn was not in Vienna at all, but in Esterház or Eisenstadt; Salieri left for Paris in the spring of this year (*Frühjahr*) says Mosel; Anfossi brought out in this same year an oratorio at Castel Nuovo, and an opera at Padua, and I can find no proof whatever that he had recently been in Vienna.

"When on the 17th of November Martín's *Cosa rara* obtained an incredible success, which, both with the public and with the Emperor, threw *Figaro* into the shade, it became possible to lay it

[2] Ibid., p. 281.

(*Figaro*) quite aside," says Jahn. Few who have read the history of Mozart have escaped the impression that Martín's opera was adopted by "Salieri and his tribe" as a means of banishing *Figaro* from the stage. To this, let it be remarked again that Salieri had been in Paris for months and that Da Ponte says: "Hardly were the parts (of the *Cosa rara*) distributed when all hell seemed to be let loose." Not knowing that the text was by him, the singers, while doing all in their power to put down Martín, praised the libretto to its author as one, which showed him how an opera should be written! Only the express command of the Emperor caused the work to be produced. The cabal had, if possible, been worse than that against Mozart, and Salieri could not possibly have borne a part in it.

Is it necessary then to believe that Salieri's intrigues kept *Figaro* from the stage? It should not be forgotten that the opposition to *Figaro* was also in a great measure led by Abbate Casti, and against Da Ponte, not against the composer; and that in less than three months after the success of *Una cosa rara*, Nancy Storace, the Susanna of *Figaro,* and O'Kelly, the Basilio, left Vienna which may well have prevented for the time a reproduction of the opera, without charging it against a man then living in Paris.

When Leopold Mozart brought his children to Vienna the second time in September, 1767, they were forced to take refuge in Olmütz on account of the ravages of smallpox, and not until January 1768, could they establish themselves in Vienna. In that month Wolfgang Mozart completed his twelfth year; Antonio Salieri entered the second half of his eighteenth. The former excited the admiration and astonishment of the Empress Maria Theresa and the musical circles of Vienna by his wonderfully precocious powers as pianist and instrumental composer, and the enmity and hatred of the routine musicians of the city, young as he was; the other was still the pupil of Gassmann, already a favorite of Joseph, and just beginning to hear compositions of his own introduced into the popular operas.

Mozart had the composition of *La finta semplice* entrusted to him, but Affligio in the end never allowed it to come to performance, nor could the Emperor command it, for at that time Affligio was the lessee of the Court stage and Joseph had no power in the premises. Intrigue and cabal conquered and the youth Salieri had no opportunity of hearing an opera from the boy Mozart.

When the Archbishop of Salzburg brought his Kapellmeister to Vienna, in March 1781, and treated him with such indignity

Catarina Cavalieri, 1786; silhouette by Hieronymus Löschenkohl. Reputedly Salieri's mistress, Cavalieri (1761-1801) sang in Mozart's *Abduction from the Seraglio,* and accompanied Salieri to a performance of *The Magic Flute* on October 13, 1791.

and cruelty as to force him to leave his service and settle in Vienna, he was in his twenty-sixth year and was already the author of some half a dozen Italian operas which had proved successes and which, though not given in Vienna, must have been known to Viennese musicians. Salieri in the meantime had produced fifteen operas, mostly for the Viennese stage and many of them with splendid success.

It is not at all improbable that the triumph of Mozart's German opera, *The Abduction from the Seraglio* (*Die Entführung aus dem Serail*) on July 12, 1782, may have opened his eyes to the surpassing genius of the young Salzburger; but it is difficult to see how any argument to prove the supposed envy and jealousy on the part of Salieri toward him can be based upon unsuccessful rivalry in the field of *German* opera, the Italian's only essay in that direction having been the *Chimney-sweeper,* which was only composed as a study—which was wretched in its text—which was produced more than a year before Mozart's work and which, in spite of the critics, was not without success.

In what was held to be his own department, Mozart was with one voice pronounced unrivalled. Who played the pianoforte with such astonishing power, sweetness, execution! Who composed concertos or, indeed, any form of chamber music which could stand the comparison with his, save indeed Prince Esterházy's Kapellmeister [Haydn] in symphony and string quartet, a man who to great and undoubted genius added the experience gained in a life which, at this time (1781-82), was double his own? It is perfectly natural that under the circumstances things should have moved on as they did. It is to us certainly a misfortune that Mozart had not two or three texts a year to compose for the stage; but his and his father's complaints, natural and well founded in one point of view as they are, should not be taken as giving us the truth, the whole truth, and nothing but the truth.

The facts as they seem to me are these: the Italian school had so long supplied the theatrical music of the court that it felt itself in the position of a possessor of a prescriptive right to furnish opera in such quantity as was desired; and where their daily bread was at stake, one cannot be surprised that the leaders of the school should exert themselves to keep out intruders. Again, after the spasmodic effort to establish German opera, during which the Italians were dismissed, Joseph returned to his first love—his only real love—and Italian opera buffa again became his evening recreation, performed by the splendid company collected by Salieri, of which Nancy Storace and the Irishman O'Kelly were members. For this company, in its third year, Mozart wrote *Figaro*. Joseph gave it a chance; but the music was no more to his taste than that of Gluck in his greater works—it did not amuse like the thin Italian scores—nor did he ever acquire a taste for so high an order of Art. *Figaro* was caviar to the general public, as were those splendid quartets which Mozart dedicated to Haydn, and, in his musical taste, the Emperor belonged to the general public. Still he gave Mozart a chance and, a year or two later when *Don Giovanni* succeeded at Prague, he had it given also in Vienna.

Dittersdorf had an interview with Joseph at this time and here is part of the conversation as he reports it:

J.—What do you think about Mozart's compositions?

D.—He is unquestionably one of the greatest original geniuses and thus far I have known no composer who possesses so astonishing a richness of ideas. I could wish he was not so prodigal of them. He does not allow the auditor to take a breath; for hardly will one reflect upon a beautiful thought, when another still finer is there, which crowds out the former and so it goes on and on until at last a man remembers not one of all these beauties.

J.—In his theatrical pieces he has the single fault that, as the singers have complained, he covers them up by his accompaniments.

D.—That would surprise me. It is very possible to introduce harmony and accompaniment without spoiling the *cantilena*.

J.—This talent you possess masterly. I have noticed it in your two oratorios *Esther* and *Job*. What do you think about Haydn's compositions?

D.—Of his operatic pieces I have heard nothing.

J.—You lose nothing thereby, for he is just like Mozart.

Since Mozart's operatic music was not to the Emperor's taste,
how was it to be expected that men whose music he did enjoy
should in his own theater be displaced to make way for him, or
that a new and unnecessary Kapellmeister-ship should be established, simply for the sake of giving a permanent situation to a
young man under thirty? A man whom the Emperor knew as the
Thalberg or Liszt of his day in his pianism, as an operatic composer who persisted in covering his scores with "too many notes"?

Again, if I have been able to read the musical history of Vienna rightly, there was not at that time a public for such works as
Figaro. True, Kelly tells us of the enthusiasm at the first performance; and so does Mozart in his letters to his father[3]; but on
the whole, it was not a work which filled the treasury of the theater. It stood as small a chance then in Vienna, when opposed to
Martín's, Dittersdorf's and Salieri's works, as it does now [1864]
in New York when opposed to Donizetti, Bellini and Verdi. Long
years after Mozart's death, when a music public had been educated by his works to a full appreciation of his almost superhuman
abilities, when his works had reformed public taste and their
influence was felt in all the operatic compositions of the age—it
was, and is, a very easy and cheap way of accounting for their
want of instant success, for the biographer and pseudomusical
historian to save himself the trouble of research and study and
heap abuse upon the scapegoat—the Imperial Kapellmeister
Salieri—finding in his envy, enmity and intrigues, a facile explanation of all the phenomena in the case.

The opinions of Prof. [Otto] Jahn upon any point connected
with Mozart are of more importance and value than those of any
other writer; and the page or two in his great work concerning
the relations between him and Salieri must find place here. It is
with very great diffidence that I confess myself not satisfied with
the final impression which these pages leave upon the mind of
the reader; it is too much like that which Holmes labors to con-
vey— though in all respects softened. As Jahn writes (III, p. 61):

> Salieri had no reason to oppose the direction of the
> Emperor's taste, since it was that which he himself fol-
> lowed. With skill and talent he sought to avail himself of
> the acquisitions made in various directions by modern

[3] Ibid., p. 282.

music, and to enable the Italian opera to meet the just demands of a refined taste. With the exception of the operas which he composed for Paris and in which he purposely adopted the style of Gluck, he in his works remained true to the traditions of the Italian opera; he introduced no substantially new element into it, and his artistic individuality was not strong and important enough to impress upon the opera a new character. But just this measure of talent, skill and taste had gained him the favor of his imperial master and the public; he would have had to possess an uncommon moral and artistic greatness of character, and independence, to have enabled him to acknowledge the newly rising genius as greater than himself, to have bowed before him and retired into the shade—and this he did not possess.

Salieri is described as a good-natured, kindly man, blameless and amiable in private life and justly honored with a reputation for noble and benevolent acts; but these good qualities could not stand the trial when they came into conflict with jealousy for his fame and his position as an artist.[?] In the year 1780 he returned to Vienna from a long journey into Italy where he had gained new honor and fame, and his hold upon the Emperor's favor was thereby only the more firmly fixed. Now he found in Mozart a rival, dangerous already through the splendor of his powers as a virtuoso which most quickly gains the loud applause of the multitude; who had by his *Abduction from the Seraglio* cast Salieri's *Chimney-sweeper* into the shade; who by his *Idomeneo* proclaimed himself a dangerous competitor in his own special field, and soon enough entered the lists with him in the Italian opera. Salieri, who would rather instinctively feel the superior strength of Mozart than clearly recognize it, could not remain entirely easy and indifferent. No misunderstanding, however, occurred in their personal relations; Mozart in his intercourse with his compeers in art was friendly, good-humored and mild in judgment, "also in respect to Salieri, who did not like

him," as Frau Sophia Haibl, his wife's sister, records;
and he (Salieri) "had too much policy" to allow his dislike of Mozart to attract attention. That this dislike really existed, that Salieri sought secretly to hinder his
rivals' advancement, was considered by Mozart's friends
and by others in Vienna as an established fact; and he
sought to injure him, not only by disparaging criticisms
in the proper quarter, but by many a little intrigue, of
which unequivocal traces will hereafter meet us [i.e. in
Jahn's volumes]. Under these circumstances, it is clear
that Salieri and Strack were allies in the music room of
the Emperor, when it was for their interest to keep out
foreign elements which must necessarily have under-
mined their long confirmed influence, in case another
direction should be given to the Emperor's taste. If,
therefore, Joseph did animate Mozart with kind words,
which gave him courage, the more so as "great people
do not like to say such things because they must always
be ready for a butcher's thrust" [an expression of
Mozart's which I do not understand—A.W.T.]—still he
had to overcome obstacles in the surroundings of the
Emperor, clearly more powerful than the favorable disposition of the monarch which Mozart was ever re-
awakening by new exhibitions of his talents. Moreover,
the economy of the Emperor came into the account,
and he could not make up his mind to add another
salary to those of the various Kapellmeisters whom he
already had in his employ.

The exact weight which should be granted to Sophia Haibl's
words, written many years after Mozart's death, and when the
idea that the young man had been the object of the bitter but
concealed enmity of Salieri had become general, is not easy to
determine. Nor need it be attempted here.

But attention must be called to one point: it seems to have
occurred to none who have had occasion to write on the relations between the two great composers, that Salieri may have
been sincerely honest in his opinions of Mozart's music. Jahn
says (III, p. 63, footnote): "I have heard from trustworthy witness-
es in Vienna that Salieri in his old age, when he thought himself

in confidential circles, expressed with a passionate emphasis painful to his hearers, the most unjust judgments upon Mozart's compositions." Mr. Joseph Hüttenbrenner has related the same thing, out of his own experience, to the present writer [Thayer]. But does that necessarily imply the personal enmity which is everywhere charged upon him? Abbé Stadler used to leave the quartet concerts in Vienna after the works of Mozart, Haydn, etc., were finished and Beethoven's came up; but there was no personal enmity. Was Sarti's notorious attack upon Mozart's six quartets dedicated to Haydn the offspring of any other feeling than zeal for what he thought the only good music? Were the French dramatic "philosophers" actuated by any base motive when they proved to their satisfaction that Shakespeare could not write a good play? Haydn's musical painting in the *Creation* was a topic for Beethoven's jocose and sarcastic remarks. Johann Peter Salomon declared in 1813 that Beethoven's Fifth Symphony was rubbish; he was perfectly honest in his opinion just as he was three years later when, in presence of the Philharmonic Society, he expressed his regret for having thus spoken, and pronounced the work what the musical world now knows it to be.[4]

Thirty years after the time of which we are now speaking, Anselm Hüttenbrenner, a very fine musician, brother of the Joseph Hüttenbrenner mentioned above, he who supported the dying Beethoven's head, became the pupil of Salieri. His reminiscences of him may be read in the Leipzig *Allgemeine Musikalische Zeitung* of November 30, 1825. A portion of this article is here introduced because it is in part directly to the purpose and in part indirectly as showing how fixed the musical views and opinions in which Hüttenbrenner was educated remained in his mind:

> Through the recommendation of Count Moritz von Fries—an in all respects magnanimous promoter of the arts—I was received in the year 1815 as a pupil in composition by the Imperial Royal Kapellmeister Salieri. The first examination to which I was subjected consisted in this: that I must sing with him a rather difficult two-part Canon, then play a Sonata of Beethoven which he placed before me, and finally extemporize. To the

---

[4] Actually, violinist/impresario Salomon died on November 28, 1815.—T.A.

question what *clefs* I was most familiar with, I replied
that all were reasonably in my power, upon which he
began to speak of the baritone and half-soprano clefs,
my ignorance of which I blushingly had to acknowledge. In his instructions in composition, Salieri
employed no textbook. He gave no directions to his
pupils concerning what they should write; each had
free choice according to his taste. What was placed
before him for correction he examined with severity.
Consecutive fifths and octaves he simply pointed out
and warned against, but a minor seventh accord in
upward motion was a thorn in his eye; and so, too, were
all progressions difficult for the singer and the so-called
relationes non harmonicae, the bad effect of which he
made us feel very sensibly by vigorously striking them
on the pianoforte. He was most rigorous in the matter
of modulation; he labored with all zeal against the constant and glaring changes of key, so common of late
years, and likened certain modern composers to people
who jump out of the window in order to get into the
street. When vocal compositions were brought to him,
he first read the words through with great attention;
then he examined the music to see whether it was written in the spirit of the text; if this was not the case,
whatever good and original passages it might possess,
the work had no sort of value in his eyes. On such occasions his zeal would grow particularly ardent, and he
would cite many passages out of the works of famous
masters who had fallen into this sort of mistake.

In compositions for the church he would have the
spirit of devotion and humility rule throughout; he
hated a pompous *Kyrie* or a jolly *Dona nobis.* In opera
(of which he himself composed fifty-two) the principal
thing was to see what character was to sing this or that
number. He complained about those composers who
have their squires sing in the same lofty style as their
knights, and in whose music the mentor quavers and
trills precisely like the pupil. He thought it also
opposed to common sense to give a rich instrumental

accompaniment to scenes of little passion; and need-
lessly to agonize the ear with barbarous accords (so he
called them) which at best could only suit a chorus of
demons. According to him the operatic composer
should not be a miniature painter and employ his
strength in the careful working out of particular figures
and in other displays of contrapuntal skill. He demanded, for the sake of the effect, strokes large and bold,
analogous to the dash of the scene painter.

He held Gluck to be the greatest operatic composer;
he alone, in his view, had best known how to express
character in music, and to produce the grandest effects
with few notes; while of late years the auditor, owing to
the lavish use of them, remained unmoved by the
mightiest masses of tones. Of Mozart he always spoke
with marked respect [*ausnehmender*—extraordinary—
Hochachtung]. He, the Unsurpassable, came often to
Salieri with the words, "Dear papa, hand me some of
the old scores out of the court library; I will look them
through here by you," and several times when thus
employed he missed his dinner. One day I asked Salieri
to show me the house in which Mozart died, upon
which he took me into the Rauhensteingasse and pointed it out. It is, if my memory serves, distinguished by a
picture of the Virgin.[5] Salieri visited him on the last day
but one of his life and was one of the few who attended
his funeral.

The "marked respect" with which Salieri always spoke of
Mozart in the presence of Anselm Hüttenbrenner, as a man of
highest genius, talent and musical learning, no doubt is perfectly
compatible with his more private explosions in relation to the
operatic music of that master. Think how Salieri's canons of criticism were invaded by Mozart! And yet in his old age Salieri could
hear no new opera which had not the Mozart style for its basis,
and which not infrequently sought success by an exaggeration of
what in the old man's eyes were Mozart's worst faults, even to car-
icature. In his view the whole direction of *opera seria* was wrong

[5] A new house called the 'Mozarthof' occupies the spot now [1864], the front ornamented with busts of several composers, and within a colossal bust of Mozart.—A.W.T.

and this tendency had been given it by Mozart's example. One can admire the greatness of "nutshell" Carlyle's genius, the extent of his acquirements, the profundity of his thoughts, and yet honestly detest his abominable use, or rather misuse of the "King's English"—as bad as Falstaff's misuse of the King's press—and despise his incapacity to perceive the truth in the cases of his heroes, or in cases where a people, and not a single individual, is heroic.

Let us for once forget all the prejudgments which we have made when reading the lamentations of Holmes, and indeed of all Mozart literature, over the success of Salieri's personal enmity and the intrigues which sprang out of it, in crushing Mozart, and look at the matter from a simple common-sense point of view, leaving romance to Polkos and soft-hearted young women—to such as really suppose that the heavens above, or the earth beneath, or the waters under the earth, can furnish, in the nineteenth century, a real original of the inane, namby-pamby Seraphiel of *Charles Auchester*.[6]

Mozart's friends claim—and justly too, as the future proved —that, when he, the young man of twenty-five, settled in Vienna, he needed but the opportunity and he would utterly cast all other composers in Vienna into the shade, would prove indisputably the overwhelming superiority of his powers, and place himself on a height beyond rivalry. Suppose Salieri perceived this—he the Imperial Royal Kapellmeister—still a young man also, and with a long career before him—he who certainly stood first as Italian operatic composer, who enjoyed the special favor of the Emperor and the Viennese public—whose works were known throughout Europe, save possibly in England—can you blame him for not at once saying: "Here, Mozart, take my scepter—true, you have not yet written any grand opera except *Idomeneo*, but I see you are a far greater genius than I am, and as you are supreme at the pianoforte and instrumental composition so make your crown triple, by adding that of Italian opera to it."

The idea thus becomes an absurdity.

---

[6] Elise Polko had published a romanticized *Erinnerungen an Felix Mendelssohn-Bartholdy*, and Elisabeth Sheppard (pseudonym: E. Berger) authored *Charles Auchester*, "a memorial to Mendelssohn," first published in England in 1853, a popular novel in the Victorian era.—T.A.

Upon the whole, the charges against Salieri—in part disproved by incorrigible and unbending dates—if not resulting in the verdict "not guilty," may at least be dismissed with the Scotch verdict "not proven." I ask for Salieri only justice—nothing more.

The *Wiener Theaterkalender* for 1787 contains a list of all the performances in the Imperial Royal Court Theater from October 1, 1785 to September 31, 1786. The theater was open 318 evenings, 157 of which were for opera, a single work, with but very few exceptions, comprising an evening's performance. For some nine months of the year opera as a rule occupied three evenings in the week; but through July and half of August opera alone was given. Salieri's *Grotta di Trofonio*—first performance, October 12, 1785—had seven representations during the first four months, three during the next five, and during the entire theatrical year seventeen. During this year his *Fiera di Venezia* was given five times, and his *Scuola de' Gelosi* twice. Mozart's *Figaro*—first performance, May 1—had six representations during the first four months, in September, October, and November, one each, when it was dropped, until revived under Salieri in 1789. His *Abduction from the Seraglio* was also given May 10 and July 21.

Paisiello was perhaps the most popular composer that year; his *King Theodore* was given eleven times, his *Barber of Seville* ten, and at least seven evenings were occupied by other works from his pen. The new operas of that theatrical year were eleven in number, in a period of ten and a half months of actual performances. One of these was the celebrated *Doctor and Apothecary* of Dittersdorf, broadly farcical, at which the theater shook with laughing, Joseph setting the example, and which had nine representations from July 11 to August 6. Another was Cimarosa's *La villanella rapita*, performed eight times from November 25, 1785 to February 17, 1786, while his *L'italiana in Londra,* revived May 17, 1786, had six representations before the close of September. The remaining 73 evenings were divided among some eighteen operas, old and new, which had from one to eight performances, and which were without exception of the buffa order. This review of the year certainly gives little encouragement to the idea that after the ninth performance of *Figaro* in November 1786, it was banished from the stage through cabal and intrigue—certainly not through an intrigue led by, or for the advantage of the absent Salieri. Except the *Grotto of Trophonius,* a work which had a very remarkable success, and was performed seventeen times in eleven months, there was no opera but *Doctor and Apothecary* which ran as many times that year as Mozart's *Figaro* from May to November.

CHAPTER 7

Paris, Axur *and Mozart's* Don Giovanni

W HILE ENJOYING THE SUCCESS of his *Grotto of Trofonius,* Salieri had another cause of high satisfaction in the reception which the printed score of *Les Danaïdes* met with from the musical world, and its renewed success in Paris. C.F. Cramer wrote him from Kiel that he "recognized throughout the score the harmonious and sensitive composer of the Enchantress Armida [i.e., Salieri's *Armida,* 1771], but at the same time one who was able, with as rapid, as unfaltering a flight, to rise above his own individual style and follow the path of Gluck, as the true and worthy heir of his mantle." [François Louis Gaud le Bland] Bailly du Roullet wrote him from Paris that the *Danaïdes* had again been put upon the stage, was listened to with delight, and applauded to the echo; that the splendid success of its first production was nothing compared to the present, and one heard but a universal cry of "What a magnificent Opera!" At the same time Bailly du Roullet asked Salieri to inform Gluck that his *Alceste* roused a higher enthusiasm with each reception.

When Salieri returned from his first Parisian visit he brought with him, as we have seen, two texts which the Academy of Music had entrusted to him for composition: *Tarare* by [Pierre-Augustin Caron de] Beaumarchais, and *Les Horaces* after Corneille, by [Nicolas-François] Guillard. After careful examination, he sent the former back to its author with remarks and requests for certain changes. Bailly du Roullet, in a letter to Salieri at this time, says: "Yesterday I called on Beaumarchais; he has received your two letters, is captivated with them, finds them full of sense and genius, and is fully determined to meet your wishes. He told me that these letters had greatly increased the respect which he feels for you, and strengthened the opinion even, which he already held of your genius and merits." Beaumarchais, having revised his text, sent it back, and Salieri devoted to it and *Les Horaces* the hours which his duties as first Kapellmeister of the Italian Opera left him free, as he says, in his own notes:

"Con grandissimo piacere, perchè il genere ragionato (il solo veramente rispettabile) a Parigi viene, generalmente parlando, sempre meglio eseguito e più gustato che altrove." ["With the greatest pleasure, because the rational form of music (the only one really respectable), generally speaking, is always better executed and more thoroughly enjoyed in Paris than anywhere else."]

Joseph in Vienna enjoyed the light opera buffa, and it was cheap. Marie Antoinette [his sister, in Paris] enjoyed the grand spectacle, and her husband spent immense sums upon it. Joseph was economical, Louis profuse. Joseph died amid the universal tears of his people. Louis and his wife lost their heads amidst the universal curses of theirs. At all events that lavishness of expense gave Salieri the opportunity of exerting his talents and genius in a higher field than Vienna opened to him since the death of Maria Theresa.

"In the spring of 1786," says Mosel, and no means is at hand for determining the date more exactly (which one would be glad to have precisely fixed, because of its bearing upon the Mozart and *Figaro* question),[1] "Salieri was invited to bring these two operas as soon as possible to Paris." Obtaining leave of absence from Joseph, he made his preparations for the journey at once. Before his departure he took a tender leave of Gluck, to whom he was mainly indebted for the fame and profit to which he was going; for with all his talents it is very doubtful if, without Gluck's recommendation, he would ever have reached the honors which had already crowned him and were awaiting him in France. Gluck, whose mother tongue was Czech (or Bohemian), expressed himself with some difficulty in German and still more so in Italian and French; and this was increased in his last years

[1] Whether anything on this point is contained in the Grimm correspondence or in that of Beaumarchais, I have not the time to go to the Library to examine.—A.W.T.

by the effects of his partial paralytic condition. He was apt to mix the three languages together in his conversation, and his parting words to his favorite protegé ran as follows:

"Ainsi—mon cher ami—lei parte domani per Parigi—Je vous souhaite—di cuore un bon voyage—Sie gehen in eine Stadt, wo man schätzet—die fremden Künstler—e lei si fará onore—ich zweifle nicht," and, embracing him, he added: "ci scriva, mais bien souvent." ("But, my dear friend, you are going away to Paris tomorrow, I wish you—pleasant journey from my heart—you are going to a city where they value—foreign artists—and you will do yourself honor—I have no doubt," and, embracing him, added: "write to me, and very often.")

It is noteworthy, adds Mosel, that Salieri has recorded these words—he who was himself in the habit in conversation of mixing the same three languages in like manner.

The first produced of his two works in Paris was *Les Horaces* [December 7, 1786], which was most favorably received by singers and orchestra at the rehearsals, and at the performance was—damned! Since the score[2] shows so many beauties as to place the work among the finest of its class, for melody, novelty of forms, beauty of the accompaniment, and adaptation to the sentiments of the text, the fall of *Les Horaces et les Curiaces* must have been owing to extraneous circumstances. Actually a concatenation of odd and unlucky accidents did occur sufficient to produce the effect with the volatile, jest-loving Parisian audience. Salieri was advised to entrust the important part of the high priest to a young man of noble person and a powerful resonant voice, but who had hitherto only sung minor parts. As a preventive against singing false he was in the habit of practicing his parts at home at a pianoforte tuned half a tone above the orchestra.

At the rehearsals he had sung exceedingly well; but at the performance, on reaching the recitative, "Le Senat rassemble sous ces voûtes sacrées," which closes the first act, notwithstanding the preceding *ritornel* of the orchestra, he began half a tone too high, as he had done at home. The act thus far had been a success, but this musical effect was too much for the audience and a burst of laughter greeted the singer from all parts of the house. The poor fellow lost his self-command and, though he found his pitch,

[2] This is according to Mosel; I know nothing about it.—A.W.T.

sang the long scene through with an uncertain voice. As a result, the curtain fell upon a cold audience. The effect upon Salieri, who sat with certain friends in a box (since the composer was not allowed in this theater to conduct his own work), may be imagined. They hoped, however, that the other two acts would be listened to more attentively, and that the opera might end with the applause with which it had in fact begun. During the progress of the second act the parterre became stiller and more attentive. Salieri was again of good courage. The scene of the finale is the field in which the Horatii and the Curiatii are to meet in mortal combat, and upon their appearance, the people, who knew of the friendly relations between the families, in their surprise at seeing them thus opposed to each other, were to shout, "Les Horaces! Les Curiaces!" Salieri had thought it best to have these words delivered without accompaniment and *ad libitum*. But at the moment one of the chorus singers, whether by mistake or for the sake of the joke, who knows? dwelt upon the syllable "Cu" (queue) in such a manner as to raise a laugh, destroy the illusion, and cause the curtain to fall upon an unsympathizing audience.

The third act passed off without gaining upon the feelings of the audience, and the exhibition of the historical fact of the murder of his sister by the only survivor of the three Horaces, brought out strong marks of disapproval.

Of course all was corrected for the next performance—the high priest sang in tune, the chorister shortened his "Cu," and the sister committed suicide—but the opera was discredited and, after three or four performances, was withdrawn.

"The result of a theatrical performance," says Salieri, commenting upon his ill success in this case, "notwithstanding all the merit a work may possess, is never to be known beforehand; but, still, it cannot be a matter of indifference to an author, unless he be a presumptuous fool."

Besides the misfortunes which had attended the first performance of this work, various imperfections in the text doubtless had their effect upon its success. It would be unjust to attribute its failure to Salieri and his music.

Salieri was soon comforted for this piece of ill fortune, and he soon forgot it except when the *Cu-riaces* came to mind as a curious and laughable jest played by chance at his expense. He was more than comforted, he was triumphant, for Beaumarchais's *Tarare,* with his music, was an almost unexampled success. I have not been able, from the authorities at hand, to fix the date of the unsuccessful work; but *Tarare* "was given," says Mosel, "soon after its fall" and the first production of this was on June 8, 1787. This is Poisot's date, as well as that given in Beaumarchais's works. Mosel gives June 7. [Angermüller confirms June 8.—T.A.]

That the two works were given with but a very short interval between, is the idea conveyed by Mosel here, but can hardly be reconciled to what has previously been said of the composer's departure from Vienna in the spring of the preceding year. It is a point of little importance except in its bearing upon the discussion of the relations between Salieri and Mozart previously given. Gerber dates *Les Horaces et les Curiaces,* 1786. Poisot does not mention it; but his work is only a sketch of Parisian musical history, and his list of operas contains only the successful ones. In this list he gives the following dates of works performed at this time in the Grand Opera:

1786, August 29. *La Toison d'or,* text, Desriaux; music, Vogel.

1787, February 1. *Oedipe á Colone,* text, Guillard; music, Sacchini.

1787, June 8. *Tarare,* text, Beaumarchais; music, Salieri.

There seems to be no room for doubt that Mosel's "soon after" must be taken *cum grano,* and that *Les Horaces* was produced in the autumn of 1786; else where could the performers have found time for its study and rehearsal? Or may it possibly have even preceded the *Toison d'or?* [As noted above, Angermüller says December 7, 1786 concerning *Les Horaces.*—T.A.]

"An analysis of the beauties of *Tarare,*" says Mosel, "would fill a book; in general it must be said that the judgment, genius, fire, the never-failing support of the action through the music, the interludes so perfectly depicting every various sentiment of the recitatives, the perfect characterization of the persons of the drama, the truth of expression in all the vocal music, and the joining all these parts into one perfect whole, raises this opera to an enduring model of its class." "Should it strike anyone as strange, that in the French opera the number of cavatinas is so large, while that of the arias is so small, let him understand," continues Mosel, "that the French (at least on the grand stage of their National Opera) demand, not a 'concert of which the drama is a pretext,' as the Abbé Amand so happily says, but a musical drama; hence no more music than serves to increase the beauty of the poem, enhance the effect of the acting, and strengthen the impression of the whole; grand arias are permitted only where their introduction will not retard the rapid progress of the action, nor jar with the feeling of the moment, but rather intensify it. Hence they require no vocal virtuosos for the performance of these works but *actors* skilled in declamatory song; and mark the difference between the French and Italian opera singers by calling the former *Acteurs chantants,* the latter *Chanteurs.*"

It must not be forgotten that Mosel wrote forty years ago and that his remarks would hardly apply to the Grand Opera of Paris since that period. [Mosel wrote in 1827, Thayer in 1864—T.A.]

At the close of the triumphant first performance of *Tarare,* both poet and composer were called for by the audience. Beaumarchais excused himself on the ground that he was but a dilettante in poetry; but two of the leading singers led Salieri forward to receive the most gratifying proofs of the general satisfaction.

This splendid result determined the directors to revive *Les Horaces,* since it was the opinion of the best judges that its fall owed to non-essential and accidental circumstances which might easily be avoided. Guillard and Salieri discussed and fixed upon the necessary alterations to be made in the text. But the political state of Paris, as the composer learned in the coffee houses and wherever he had an opportunity to observe the condition of public opinion, rendered him anxious to be again in the peaceful circle at home; and this desire was stronger than his craving for fame and profit, which a successful reproduction of the unlucky work would certainly have brought him.

He took leave of Paris, therefore, promising the Directors to compose at home and forward to them the new music made necessary by the alterations decided upon. But the Revolution broke out and this plan broke down. So that was the end of *Les Horaces.*

Shortly before leaving Paris, Salieri went out one afternoon from his lodgings (in Beaumarchais's house) to make some calls, intending to spend the evening in a private concert. Since the

latter was postponed, instead of accepting the invitation of a
friend to pass the evening with him in some other place, an inex-
plicable feeling led him to return to his lodgings, where he
found his servant on the floor at the point of death, suffocated
by the fumes of charcoal. The man's life was thus saved by merest
accident. Had not the gentleman who was to have given the concert been taken ill, Henry would have died.

The Duke of Aremberg invited Salieri to visit him at Brussels;
whether this invitation was accepted Mosel cannot determine;
but that he left Paris in the middle of September is clear from his
having received a letter from Beaumarchais, dated the 18th of
that month; and other circumstances seem to prove that he was
back in Vienna as early as July.

His first work there was the composition of *Le jugement dernier*
[The Last Judgment], a cantata, text by Chevalier Roger, for the
Société d'Appolon at Paris, which had applied to him for something expressly composed for its concerts. Count d'Ogny—probably the president of the Society—to whom Salieri dedicated the
work, caused the story to be circulated before the performance,
that it was a joint production of Gluck and Salieri. The object was
to stop the mouths of certain critics who swore by Gluck, and
who thus were led to declare sublime much that they otherwise
would have found at best mediocre. After a distinguished success
had crowned the work, the Count published the following "correction" in the Parisian journals:

> A public statement, based upon erroneous informa-
> tion, has been made that the music of the cantata, *Le
> jugement dernier,* is by Gluck and Salieri. It is by Salieri
> alone. It is no more than just to secure to this skillful
> composer the fame and merit of having created a work,
> so beautiful and so judiciously conceived in all its parts.
> In the subject of this cantata great difficulties had to be
> overcome; the greatest was, doubtless, that of introduc-
> ing the Divine Lawgiver as actually speaking. Monsieur
> Salieri, however, solved this problem to the extraordi-
> nary satisfaction of every auditor. The moment, in
> which the presence of God in all his majesty was
> announced, excited a feeling of awe; the music of the
> righteous and of the damned produced the highest

effect; in a word, this work, as original as it is splendid,
raises the fame of Salieri to a still higher degree.

Then follows praises of [Henri-Joseph] Rigel, the conductor, of
the vocalists and the orchestra.

De Gouve, whether with more politeness or truth, who can
now decide? wrote from Paris that this cantata, in spite of the
Italians, who decried it, "had turned the heads of all the world;"
that Rigel, who conducted, had been so excited by it as to
become ill; and that Gossec could not get over his astonishment
at the successful manner in which Salieri had made the Saviour
speak!

Count d'Ogny wrote in a similar strain and accompanied his
warmest thanks with the information that the cantata had been
twice given in the *Concert olympique* and twice in the *Concert spir-*
ituelle, each time with the same splendid result; and that he had
intended to send him a golden snuff-box but, owing to the trouble of forwarding such presents into foreign lands, he was now
on the point of sending him instead, 600 francs.

Roger, author of the text, wrote him in relation to the production of the work in the *Concert spirituelle*:

"A subject so imposing as that of the Last Judgment, and a
fame like that of the composer of *Tarare* and the *Danaïdes,* awakened in the mind of the public the idea of something astounding
and beyond the reach so to speak, of art. Where the expectations
are raised so high it is seldom that the greatest work can satisfy
them; nor did you receive the full meed of that applause which
you merited. The work was listened to with the closest attention.
The introduction, which seemed to me in the *Concert olympique*
rather tame, left on this occasion nothing to be desired, as the
effect was heightened by a moderate use of the bass drum. The
choruses are finely grouped together, and reflect the sense of the
words perfectly. I had intended an occasional interruption of
them by short recitatives, but now feel that these recitatives gain
breadth and effect by being chorally treated. Your accompaniment to the strophe 'Prends pitié de notre misère' is something
entirely new. As I wrote, I supposed I was giving you a subject
similar to that of 'Avec tes decrets infinis,' etc., in *Tarare.* You
have shown me, however, that new founts are ever opening to
genius and that it never repeats itself. The chorus 'Reveil

funeste' seems to me to be of perfect beauty. The passage 'O montagnes, écrasez-nous!' during which thunder announces the coming of the Saviour, produced a great effect, an effect truly appalling. You have given the sentences of the Supreme Judge with an indescribably enchanting effect, one which is felt equally by the skilled and the unskilled in music. The first question of Gossec, when he heard that the *Last Judgment* was to be performed, was: 'Is Christ introduced as speaking?' Yes. 'Then,' he replied, 'it is impossible that the work can succeed. I have refused to compose that subject because I felt the impossibility of giving the Son of God any adequate language.' Since hearing your work, Gossec's opinion has changed completely, and what before seemed to him an unavoidable rock of offence, has become the principal subject of his admiration in your work. I come now to the double chorus which closes the Cantata. It is beyond my comprehension why it is less prominent than it should be; the contrast is well managed, the different emotions correctly expressed: perhaps the continuous effect of the two preceding numbers weakens that of this, which in fact leaves the auditor too cold at the point where he should be excited with delight by the song of the blessed, and with awe at that of the damned. A musician of well-known talents was of opinion that the choruses are too soon interwoven in one; he would have preferred to hear the contrasting themes first given separately. You better than anyone else can judge of the value of this remark. I must here also confess something to you which is too generally felt to be passed over in silence. The signal at which all created beings start again in life seemed by no means imposing enough; it is not in sufficient contrast to the general tone of the rest of the composition. Be it that the orchestra too soon covers the trumpet blasts with its accords, or that the related key of D minor follows that of F too naturally, instead of this passage having a bold, unexpected modulation, as if independent of all rules, the only surprise in it was to hear the words sung, 'Quel signal effrayant!' ('What a frightful signal!'), when in fact no one was at all frightened. This, sir, is the only fault in your Oratorio which, except in this, I hold to be a masterpiece; a fault which would at once have been mended had you been present at the performance."

Mosel adds: "Although the too sharply expressed criticism upon the finale of the cantata is not entirely without foundation still, as a whole, it belongs to the very best works of Salieri, and would never fail of producing its intended effect when performed in the true spirit of the composition. To give a greater chance of usefulness, before the close of the composer's life, the text was carefully translated into German, and Salieri himself adapted it to the music."

I find no record of its performance since. [A.W.T.]

While engaged in the composition of this work, to be precise, on the 11th of November, 1787, Salieri called upon Gluck to discuss with him the question of how he should introduce Christ as speaking. He asked the old master if he could approve his plan of writing the part in high tenor, on the ground that the work was for Paris where that voice, with the clef and under the name of contralto was in common use, while it, moreover, was more penetrating than any other. Gluck justified his intention and added, half in jest and half in earnest: "I shall in a short time be able to inform you with certainty from the other world in what clef the Saviour speaks." On the 15th, four days afterward, another attack of apoplexy closed Gluck's life.

The distress of Salieri at the loss of Gluck was to some extent assuaged by the reports of his own increasing fame which reached him from Paris.

Blumendorf, a member of the Austrian Legation in that city, wrote him in December, 1787, that *Tarare* had already been given twenty-four times with the same applause and would be kept on the stage until Easter.

Rauquit-Lieutaud informed him that fans and snuff-boxes "a la *Tarare*" were for sale in the shops and that 4,500 livres, his share in the profits of the opera, were already on deposit for him.

Du Buisson—was this the chevalier of that name who was aide de camp of Baron de Kalb at the battle of Camden in our Revolution?—had made a French translation of Salieri's *Scuola de' gelosi*, and was now laboring to have it brought out in Paris while at the same time the Versailles operatic company was rehearsing the *Grotta di Trofonio*. Du Buisson had also written a text, *Bellerophon*, for him which, however, Salieri never composed.

Arnault wrote him that he had made the changes suggested by

him in his *Sappho* and had read it to the Committee of the
Opera, and that no remark had been made upon it. While he, "a
second Pygmalion," expressed his impatience to have "this, his
Galatea, soon made alive by the master's music," he also wrote
that the Italian company in Paris was preparing to bring out two
of his operas—which ones, however, he had forgotten. Du Roger
wrote him of the production of Paisiello's *King Theodore in Venice,*
criticizing it very severely as Beaumarchais had done in September. The latter had written to Salieri: "It is impossible, without
sighing over the fall of the Italian composers, to see the musical
art so degraded. There is no common sense in it;" and now Du
Roger says he cannot conceive how Moline can have prevailed
upon the directors to bring out a work so opposed to the principles of the Grand Opera. He goes on to speak of the continued
success of *Tarare,* and takes occasion to say: "Without intending
mere compliment to you, it requires no small faculty to be able
with such a subject to fix our attention through three full hours;
it would have been much simpler to have escaped being tedious.
Let me set it as a task to all the Italian composers who have been
or still are; they would never effect it with all their melody. Gluck
and you have gained us a great advantage over them."

♯ ♯ ♯ ♯ ♯

"About the time that Mozart returned [from Prague, after
bringing out *Don Giovanni* there—A.W.T.] to Vienna, Gluck died.
Perhaps the success of *Don Giovanni* in Prague had its effect in
inducing Emperor Joseph to keep Mozart in Vienna, who had
earnestly thought of emigrating to London, by appointing him
chamber musician by patent of December 7, 1787. Probably the
production of *Don Giovanni* would have benefitted him, but for
the present that was not to be thought of." In June 1787, Salieri
had brought out his opera *Tarare* in Paris, in which Beaumarchais had not only by means of a plot exciting and full of action,
of splendid decorations and costumes, sought to work upon the
public, but also through political and philosophical doctrine, as
where, for instance, in the strange allegorical prologue he makes
the Genius of Fire and Nature sing:

Mortal, whatever you may be, prince, brahmin [priest] or soldier,
Man, your greatness on this earth

Despends not upon your situation.

It rests in your character.

"The audience was at first somewhat puzzled and found the music much weaker than that of the *Danaïdes*, produced three years before; but the splendor of the performance and no doubt also the singular mingling of heterogeneous elements which the course of events at that time produced, had a great effect and made the piece 'draw.'

"The Emperor Joseph, whom the music greatly pleased, ordered Da Ponte to make an Italian translation, and that the opera should be given in Vienna at the celebration of the marriage of Archduke Franz and princess Elisabeth of Württemberg. This Italian opera, *Axur*, retained the plot in its principal incidents, but both in respect of text and music was completely changed. All the political and philosophical elements were excluded, and those of intrigue and sentiment in the action were reformed in the regular routine of the Italian opera. Da Ponte again showed his great skill, while Salieri evidently found here a more congenial field [than when composing the French original—A.W.T.], and engaged in the work of rewriting the music without reluctance. As he was making every possible effort to eclipse the splendid success which Martín's *Arbore di Diana* had had in the autumn, he could not be willing to risk any dangerous competitor before the production of his work. *L'amor costante* of [Domenico] Cimarosa had no success and was not a dangerous rival, but Mozart's *Don Giovanni*, most favorably heralded by the enthusiasm of the Prague public, threatened again to revive the hardly silenced applause which *Figaro* had called out."

The above is from Jahn's *Mozart*, IV, 305-06. Passing over what Jahn adds about the production and success of *Axur*, and its popularity in all Germany, I [Thayer] translate the following bitter sentences against Salieri.

"It was now advisable to allow the favorable disposition of the public [toward Salieri] to strengthen itself and not be drawn in any other direction through the production of any great work. Therefore *Don Giovanni* must not be allowed performance; Mozart might produce dances for the amusement of the Viennese," etc., etc., etc. "But Joseph II, who was pleased with the success of *Don Giovanni* in Prague, had ordered its production, and so at last the work had to be undertaken. On May 7, 1788, *Don Giovanni* was given and was unsuccessful."—But only at first, for as it was repeated at short intervals, May 7, 9, 12, 23, 26, 30, June 16, 23, July 6, 11, 21, 31, the Viennese were forced "to chew upon it," as Mozart said to Da Ponte, and soon found it to their taste.

I have not the assurance to decide that Jahn here does injustice to Salieri. No man has so studied the history of Mozart as that writer; no man's judgment is so weighty in all questions relating to him—and yet it is impossible for me to see this matter in the same light. In justice to Jahn, I have given completely here what he says about the point in question. That which makes me hesitate to accept his view is three-fold: a consideration of the dates of production, the words of Da Ponte, and the narrative of Salieri himself.

The new Italian operas of 1787-88 were:

1787, April 9.	*L'inganno amoroso.*	Guglielmi
	May 7. *Le trame deluse.*	Paisiello
	May 25. *Le stravagante inglese*	Bianchi
	June 22. *Il Bertoldo.*	Piticchio
	July 28. *Le due contesse*	Paisiello
	October 1. *L'arbore di Diana*	Martín
	November 13. *L'amor costante*	Cimarosa
1788, January 8.	*Axur Re d'Ormus*	Salieri
	April 21. *La modista*	Paisiello
	May 7. *Don Giovanni*	Mozart
	June 2. *Le gelosie fortunate*	Anfossi
	July 15. *Gli amanti canuti*	Anfossi
	August 10. *Il fanatico burleto.*	Cimarosa
	September 10. *Il talismano*	Salieri
	November 14. *Il pazzo per forza*	Weigl

Thus in 1787, seven new operas, either written for Vienna or imported from the theaters in Italy, were studied and brought out; and in the next year eight; the first of which, however, belonged in composition, study and rehearsal to the former year. One has but to reflect that *Don Giovanni* was not written for Vienna, while *L'arbore di Diana* and *Axur* were, and that too by command of the Emperor, and that the latter was ordered for an occasion the date of which was not yet fixed and which, for aught Salieri could know, might have come several weeks earlier—to see that the operatic company was fully occupied, without adding to its labors the sublime score of the greatest of all operas! It certainly does seem to me that Jahn has followed prejudice rather than judgment in the above given strictures upon Salieri. Had Salieri been Mozart's most intimate friend, could he have brought out an opera written for Prague and first given there October 23, one day earlier than it really was given? Could he have interrupted the studies of the actors upon a work, which by the command of his master he was furnishing to them, as we shall see, in vocal score alone, from want of time to add the instrumentation?

Let us turn to Da Ponte—whose reminiscences, written thirty years afterward, four thousand miles away from all means of correcting lapses of memory, are often confused in order of time and sometimes mistaken in facts—but which in this case are easily corrected when necessary.

Da Ponte, having wasted time in writing *Il filosofo punito* [*confuso*] for Righini, *Il Bertoldo* for Piticchio, and a new text to an old opera of Brunati, all of which failed, was thus admonished, as he tells us, by the Emperor: "Da Ponte, write only for Mozart, Martini [Martín] and Salieri, but never again have anything to do with such paltry, ignorant people as these. Casti was craftier than you—he wrote no operas but for a Paisiello or a Salieri."

"I now thought it time," says the old poet, "to awaken my poetic vein again, which seemed to me quite dried up, when attempting to write for Righini and Piticchio. The three above named Kapellmeisters, Mozart, Martini [Vincent Martín y Soler], and Salieri, gave me the opportunity for this, for at the same time they each demanded an opera of me, and I hoped not only to gain from all three amends for my previous failures, but even an addition to the small theatrical reputation which I had already gained. I reflected whether I might not satisfy all three at the same time—whether I might not write three operas at once. Salieri demanded no original drama. He had written the opera *Tarare* for Paris, and now desired to re-write it both in character and music as an Italian drama; therefore he called upon me for a free translation. Mozart and Martini left me free choice in the subject; I chose for the former *Don Giovanni*, which pleased him to an extraordinary degree, and for the latter *L'arbore di Diana.*"

"On the first day, what with the Tokay, Seville snuff, coffee, the servant's bell, and the young nurse [a beautiful but frail damsel of seventeen, with whom the poet was at first only *paternally* in love—A.W.T.], the first two scenes of *Don Giovanni,* two others of the *L'arbore di Diana,* and more than half of the first act of *Tarare,* a title which I had changed into *Axur, re d'Ormus,* were finished. The next morning I took these scenes to the three composers who could hardly believe what they saw and read with their own eyes; and in sixty-three days the first two operas were finished, and more than two thirds of the other. The *L'arbore di Diana* was the first which was produced (October 1). It enjoyed the happiest reception, one which was at least as good as that of the *Cosa rara.*"

"Immediately after the first performance, I was obliged to journey to Prague where Mozart's *Don Giovanni* was to be given for the first time, upon the arrival of the Princess of Tuscany in that city. I remained there eight days to instruct the actors who were to appear in the work, but before the performance, I was forced to return to Vienna by a most urgent letter from Salieri, in which he wrote me—whether truly or not I shall not decide—that *Axur,* by imperial command, was to be immediately produced on occasion of the marriage of Archduke Franz, and that the Emperor himself had ordered him to recall me. I returned, therefore, as soon as possible, traveling day and night,"—and in two or three days was again in Vienna, where in two days more, he says, *Axur* on his part was perfected. By this account, then, Salieri received the remainder of his text just as *Don Giovanni* was appearing upon the stage in Prague (October 29).

There seems to be no reason whatever to doubt the truth of this story of Da Ponte and, taking it in connection with other fixed dates, the combination enables us to fix pretty conclusively the time of Salieri's return from Paris and the beginning of the *Axur.*

Da Ponte's *Il Bertoldo,* with Piticchio's music, failed June 22; and this event preceded the conception of the *Don Giovanni* and the *L'arbore di Diana.* Mozart was ready in September to journey to Prague, that he might finish his composition in communication with his singers; and Martín had his opera ready for rehearsal early enough to secure its performance on October 1.

The writing of these two texts by Da Ponte was finished in sixty-three days; allowing then four weeks for the study of the *Arbore*, we are able to fix upon the beginning of July 1787, as the date of the conception of three of the most popular operas of that time—one of them of all time; a date, too, which allows Salieri some four weeks between the production of his *Tarare* in Paris on June 8, and his reappearance in Vienna.

Mosel gives us the history of *Axur* from Salieri's own papers. The composer and poet began their labor as a mere translation—obeying in this Joseph's order. Three or four mornings they had wrought thus in company, but with little satisfaction in their work, as both doubted the possibility of its success in Vienna. "The music," says Salieri "being composed for the French singing actors, was everywhere too wanting in melodies for the Italian acting singers. When the poet was satisfied with his verses, the music—to use the expression of Gluck—tasted too much of translation; and when to satisfy my ear, the text was adapted to the finished music, Da Ponte was displeased with his poetry. In my anxiety lest we both should labor in vain, I chose rather to compose new music to the same subject. I therefore asked the poet to plan a poem on the basis of the French original, but suited to the Italian Opera Company, and to arrange the various vocal pieces in concurrence with me, while as to the versification he should follow his own taste: I would see to the rest." Da Ponte accepted the proposition. They began anew. Poet and composer went hand in hand. When a musical idea in *Tarare* could be used, Salieri adopted it; when this was not the case, he composed the music afresh.[3] A rheumatic disease of his knee compelled Salieri for some three weeks to keep to his room, and thus, by relieving him from all his duties in the theater, enabled him to devote his whole time to the *Axur* and hasten its completion. As another means of gaining time, he composed the scenes as Da Ponte brought them, one by one, at first for the voices and the instrumental bass, and sent them in this condition to the copyist, that they might be put into the hands of the vocalists sooner. Joseph—learning that three acts were already finished, not knowing however in what manner the composer had wrought, but

[3] As noted below, *Tarare* and *Axur* are compared in parallel columns in Mosel, *Salieri*, pp. 98-112.—T.A.

supposing a mere translation of the French text had been made by the poet and adapted to the music by Salieri—desired to have what was ready in his usual afternoon concerts. He had the manuscript brought him from the copyist and the usual musicians called together. They soon noticed that the scores contained nothing but the vocal parts, with here and there a *ritornel* as a hint for the accompaniment, and the rest of the staves for the instrumentation were vacant. They mentioned this to Joseph, who replied, "That's no matter; we have the printed score of the French opera; the instruments can be played out of that and the others can sing with me at the pianoforte out of the Italian manuscript."

So each took his place. The Emperor, sitting at the pianoforte, began: "Act 1, scene 1, Duet."

"The French opera begins with a prologue," was the reply.

"They have probably omitted that in the translation," answered Joseph, "turn to the first scene."

"Here," said the musicians, "it begins with a dialogue in recitative."

"In my copy," returned the monarch, "the opera begins with a duet, which serves as an introduction, followed by an aria and then by a short duet."

"In our score," said the musicians, "there is nothing of all that to be found."

Nearly two hours were spent in examining and comparing, without finding anything that was exactly the same in the two scores; and the fruit of all their pains was at last the discovery occasionally of a similar musical thought, which, however, was generally in another key and introduced in an entirely different connection with the others. At last Joseph exclaimed, laughing: "It is enough to make one crazy! What in the world have the two been about! Go to Salieri," turning to Kreibig, "and tell him of the pretty comedy we have been playing." Kreibig [or Kreibich—A.W.T.] came the same evening to the composer, told him the story, and added that the Emperor was not satisfied with the alterations he had undertaken. A day or two later Salieri was able to go again to the palace. As soon as Joseph saw him, he began, "I am glad to see you well again. Day before yesterday you brought us almost to despair with your music. Tell me though, why you have so completely changed your French music?"

Upon Salieri's explaining (as above given) the reasons for this, not only were they deemed sufficient, but Joseph, after the performance, "praised the work and gave the composer an imperial reward for the pains he had taken."

The haste with which Da Ponte had been recalled from Prague before the production of *Don Giovanni*—an order which as salaried Court Poet he could not disobey—proved unnecessary. The marriage ceremony of the Archduke Franz was to be performed by his uncle, Maximilian Franz, the young Elector and Archbishop of Cologne; but he did not leave Bonn until December 11, 1787, and was nine days on the way. Then came the Christmas holidays, so that the wedding was put off until January 6, 1788—and of course with it the production of *Axur*. When given, it proved in its new form as splendid a success in Vienna as it had been in Paris in its old. It was given twenty-nine times during the year, notwithstanding—as shown by the list above given—seven other new Italian operas were studied and brought out by November 14, the second of them being *Don Giovanni*. A sufficient reason why Mozart's opera did not immediately follow the *Axur* may also be found in the taste of Joseph for the pure opera buffa—which taste was gratified by the production of Paisiello's *La modista*—not to mention the inhumanity, it might almost be called, of demanding the troupe to study and rehearse Mozart's mighty score immediately after the great labor of bringing out Salieri's greatest work.

Axur immediately went the round of the Italian opera houses in Germany, and in a poor translation was, within some two years, on all the principal national stages also. It was one, if not the last, of the operas in which Ludwig van Beethoven, viola player in the Bonn orchestra, could have performed his part before leaving his native city forever.

The story told by Kreibich to Salieri of the attempted rehearsal in Joseph's music-room of the unfinished music of *Axur* is fully borne out by the long parallel which Mosel [pp. 98-112] gives of *Tarare* and *Axur*. The overture and an aria or two are about all that is unchanged. The critic, who in the Berlin *Musikalisches Wochenblatt* (October 1791), says, after the performance of *Axur* at Potsdam: "Still a large portion of the music composed for the

French text remains," should inform us what he understands by the term "a large portion." He, however, praises the work very highly indeed. "On the whole," he concludes, "this music produces an effect which can only be felt, and admits not of description; and it might properly be reckoned among the very best of its class, if it was not here and there a little too rhapsodical."

Mosel says: "The opera *Axur* not only shares all these combined excellences [those mentioned above as distinguishing *Tarare*], but surpasses them in that, without diminishing any one of them, the melody is still more prominent, captivating, and penetrating than in *Tarare.* It may therefore be boldly affirmed that *Axur* is the most excellent of all serious Italian operas—Mozart's *Clemenza di Tito* included—that is, be it carefully remarked, as a dramatic tone-work, and not as a vocal composition in the wider sense of the term."

In April 1788, old Bonno died at the age of seventy-eight, and Salieri was appointed his successor as Imperial Royal Kapellmeister—a place to which he was certainly entitled, and of which he was worthy, if long and successful service as director and composer could give him a title or render him worthy. If this appointment was made directly after Bonno's decease, the patent must have been ready some time previously, as the Emperor left Vienna on February 29 for the camp in the war against the Turks, and did not see his capital again until December 5. His office gave him two hundred ducats ($1250? [in 1864 dollars]) more salary (according to Gerber's *Lexikon der Tonkünstler*), but added much to his labors, for he had now the direction not only of the Opera but also of the sacred music in the palace chapel.

If the patent, as I suspect, was dated in April, we have the significant fact that his first duty as chief Kapellmeister was to bring out Mozart's *Don Giovanni*—for Paisiello's *La modista* was already rehearsed so as to be produced on April 21—and that at this very time he himself had finished a new opera, *Cublai,* [*gran kan de Tartari*], text by Casti, which he had not power nor influence enough to put upon the stage—neither then nor at any subsequent period.

Another sentence from Jahn (*Mozart,* IV, p. 307), immediately following what has been above cited in relation to the production of *Don Giovanni*, belongs here, and is as follows: "But Joseph II, who was much pleased with the success of *Don Giovanni* in Prague, had commanded the performance [of it in Vienna], and so at last it had to be taken in hand." If Salieri and his partisans were the cause that Mozart's opera had not been given previously during the Emperor's presence in Vienna, is it not a very curious circumstance that now, when at the head of the Italian theater, Salieri, with the aid of his allies, was unable, in the absence of the monarch, to suppress it entirely and produce his own new work in its stead? Fourteen times during Joseph's absence *Don Giovanni* was performed and once (December 15, 1788) after his return. But whether he—mostly confined to his bed as he was—ever heard that opera is a point I am unable to determine.

And here, I think, the close of our discussions of the relations between Mozart and Salieri—save a fact or two which will come in their proper places—is reached. I cannot, however, dismiss the matter without a further remark or two.

1. Mozart writes to his father on July 2, 1783, [see Nissen, pp. 474-75; Holmes, American edition, pp. 239-40; Jahn, III, pp. 276-77; (Anderson No. 494—T.A.)] that, having composed a rondo for the tenor [Johann Valentin] Adamberger to introduce into Anfossi's, *Il curioso indiscreto*, Salieri, at a rehearsal, took the singer aside and told him that Count Orsini-Rosenberg [the general manager] would not like it if he introduced an aria, and as a friend advised him not to do it; and that in consequence of this "tour," or trick, the rondo was omitted. Of the bare fact in this case there can be no question. True, it rests upon Mozart's letter alone; but he was a man of truth. It should, however, not be forgotten that on this occasion the German songstress, [Aloysia Weber] Lange, sister of Mozart's wife—who did introduce two arias—and Adamberger, the German tenor, made their first appearance on the Italian stage, thus invading a territory which had belonged almost exclusively to the Italians. It was the most natural thing in the world that the Italians, young Salieri and all, should make common cause in the work of keeping the Italian opera in their own hands and not allowing the Germans from the Kärntnertor [Theater] to drive them from the stage of the Burg [Theater]. It was equally natural that Mozart should put the worst construction upon the affair, and suppose that Salieri

was the "head and front" of the offense of not allowing him opportunity to exhibit the talents he was conscious of possessing.

2. Mozart's suspicions of Salieri seem to have had their origin in an occurrence soon after his settlement in Vienna in 1781. The Princess of Württemberg, the bride of Archduke Franz, had come to Vienna to have the advantages of the capital in completing her education, and Mozart applied through Archduke Maximilian (afterward Elector of Cologne) for the position of her music teacher. Maximilian, says Jahn (*Mozart,* III, p. 49), "applied at once to the Princess. ..., but received the answer that if it depended upon her she should have chosen him; but the Emperor—'with him there is nothing but Salieri!' writes Mozart, fretfully—had proposed Salieri for the sake of her singing, whom she therefore must take, for which she was very sorry."

Knowing as we do the relations between Joseph and Salieri and the latter's very great talents and acquirements in the vocal art, is it possible to conceive that the Emperor should pass him by and give the appointment to the young emigrant from Salzburg? But that the next year Mozart could not obtain the place of teacher of the pianoforte to the Princess owing to the opposition of Salieri, seems to be the fact and one which is to the discredit of the Italian.

Finally. Da Ponte nowhere hints at any misunderstanding between the two composers nor at any efforts of Salieri to hinder the production of either *Figaro* or *Don Giovanni.* Yet he, Da Ponte, was a friend and even protegé, as well as countryman, of Salieri; and it certainly would not have been difficult for the Imperial Royal Kapellmeister to have exerted some decisive influence upon his countryman, the Imperial Royal Court Poet, and to have hindered him from giving Mozart two such splendid subjects for the exhibition of his talents, as those two greatest of Italian operas.

And now let a few lines from Holmes (pp. 227-28), of which the reader may believe as much as he pleases or his judgment will let him, conclude this matter:

"The most active and inveterate against Mozart of all the Italian clique was Salieri. This composer, whose talents were just sufficient to enable him to live in some estimation, was a creature of Gluck's. Salieri had been with that master in Paris [a mistake—

A.W.T.], and to him Gluck confided the libretto of his opera [mistake No. 2—A.W.T.] of the *Danaïdes*, the work with which he intended to close his own labors, when an attack of apoplexy made him suddenly cease writing and consult the preservation of his health in retirement."

Then in a note Holmes adds:

"Salieri imitated the style of Gluck in his *Tarare* and other works which are now, according to the usual fate of imitations, forgotten. As this composer has long been notorious for his animosity against Mozart, some personal description may not be unwelcome. The mother of the celebrated Signora [Anna (Nancy)] Storace, who saw him repeatedly in Vienna, described him as a little man with an animated countenance and peculiarly fine eyes, and his appearance altogether strongly reminded her of [actor David] Garrick."

These passages from Holmes remind one of St. Paul's words: "For I hear them record that they have a zeal of God, but not according to knowledge."

NOTE:—Würzbach, in his *Biographisches Lexikon des Kaiserthums Österreich*, article on "Joseph II," gives the following dates for the year 1788:

<pre>
January 6. . . . . Marriage of Archduke Franz
February 9 . . . . War declared against the Turks
February 29. . . . . Emperor's departure for the army
March 14 . . . . His arrival at Semlin
April 24. . . . . Taking of Sabacz
August 7 . . . . Turkish invasion of the Banat
August 27 . . . . Taking of Dubicza
September 20 . . . . Retreat from Caransches
September 29 . . . . Taking of Choczim
October 3. . . . . Taking of Novi
December 5. . . . . Joseph's return to Vienna
</pre>

I [Thayer] have consulted several authorities, all of which confirm the absence of Joseph through all this season. What is to be said, then, to Da Ponte's story in form following:

"The Emperor sent for me [after his return from Prague— A.W.T.] and, while he overwhelmed me with the most flattering expressions, made me a present of another hundred ducats and said he had a great desire soon to hear *Don Giovanni*. Mozart came back and gave his score instantly to the copyists, who has-tened to write out the parts because the Emperor was soon to leave Vienna. The opera came to performance—and shall I say it?—*Don Juan did not please!* Everybody, except Mozart, thought it defective. Additions were made, entire arias were changed, it was again brought out—and *Don Giovanni did not please!* And what said the Emperor thereto? 'The opera is exquisite—is divine—perhaps better even than the *Figaro,* but it is no meat for the teeth of my Viennese.' I told Mozart this expression, who answered me with perfect calmness, 'Time must be given them to chew upon it.' He did not deceive himself. By his advice I caused it to be often repeated, and with each performance the applause increased," etc., etc.

It is impossible to think that Da Ponte invented this story. Was there, then, a private performance in the winter? How can the story be reconciled to the fact that Joseph was not in Vienna at the public production of *Don Giovanni?* The most rational hypothesis is that Da Ponte, writing after thirty years had elapsed, supposed a remark really made in the Emperor's afternoon con-cert over the score, to have been made after the public perfor-mance of *Don Giovanni* in the theater.

CHAPTER 8

At the Height of Fame

SALIERI, WHO HARDLY EVER knew a day's sickness until some seventy years of age, has left us one little picture of his family life, at the time he was confined to his bed with the rheumatic trouble in his knee before mentioned, January 1788.[1]

"My wife," said the composer, "usually sat with two of my daughters, working at a table by my bedside; my son was busy at my writing desk with his studies; two younger daughters were in the next room knitting and in charge of the three youngest girls, who played with their dolls; I lay in bed and, in the intervals of reading and thinking, enjoyed this, for me, exquisite sight. At seven o'clock my wife and children performed aloud their evening devotions and then again proceeded with their various employments. At a later hour my son took his seat at the pianoforte and, if either of his sisters wished it he would play a waltz and the girls danced in merry round. At nine o'clock my wife and a maid came to steam or smoke my lame leg or whatever else the physician had ordered. One of the oldest girls then brought me my soup, and half an hour later my wife, son, and my seven daughters came—she giving me a kiss, the others kissing my hand, to wish me a good night. How pleasantly in this wise flew the evenings! How quickening to the heart of a fond husband and father is such an enjoyment!"

Poor Salieri! His wife, son, and three daughters went before him to the grave; the loss of his only son was especially bitter and one he often mourned over in his latter years.

Perhaps nowhere better than here can a word be introduced

---

[1] Here is again a date which does not correspond well to the story of the composition of *Axur*, as given before; but Mosel had a happy talent for mixing dates as his sketch of Salieri's life in several places abundantly shows.—A.W.T.

upon Salieri's love of nature. In this regard he was like Beethoven with, however, a characteristic difference. Beethoven delighted in long rambles over the hills and in the deep valleys among the mountains which approach within a few miles of the capital. Unmarried and unconfined by any official or family duties, he could indulge this taste—in his case rising to the strength of a passion—to its fullest extent. Salieri, tied by his duties as Kapellmeister and enjoying the sweets of a happy family life, had his favorite walks near the city on the broad, flat island of the Danube which, at is upper end, is called the Brigittenau; which, immediately opposite the city, is partially covered with the suburb, Leopoldstadt, with its fine public garden called the Augarten and which then spreads away for some miles in the public grounds known as the Prater. ("So jolly as in the Prater," says Mephistopheles to Faust.) Beethoven's stormy nature delighted in mountains and woods; Salieri's gentler feelings found play in the broad, green spaces and scattered groves of the plain. Beethoven delighted in looking down from the heights; Salieri in contemplating the heights themselves from below. Let him tell the story of his three favorite trees.

"Many years ago I had selected three noble trees, standing apart, for my favorites, under whose cool shade I passed many a happy hour in reading, composing, and reflection. One of them stands in the Prater, the second in the Augarten, and the third in the Brigittenau. The view from the first embraced to the right an arm of the Danube and wooded islands beyond; to the left, broad reaches of greensward adorned with wild rose bushes and handsome groups of young trees; while in front the eye looked across plains and valleys away to Leopoldsberg and Kahlenberg, both crowned with romantic old cloisters.

"The second of my trees was in the Augarten, thickly surrounded with bushes various in sort and size, between which I could see at a distance the people as they strolled through the various avenues. From the third tree I saw to the right, hills and valleys—abodes of men; to the left, thick woods; in front the river and a superb view of the city and its suburbs. How many happy hours I lived under these three majestic trees! The dreadful hurricane of [October 1] 1807 caused them, it may be said, to disappear; that in the Prater and that in the Brigittenau, in spite of

their size, were torn up by the roots with a thousand others; that
in the Augarten split down to within a man's height of the
ground. Two days after that raging storm I saw and shuddered at
the terrible devastation. True, there were still pleasant spots
enough left in those lovely groves but, as I was so accustomed on
every first of May to spend at least half an hour under my
favorite trees—yes, even in winter time, and especially in March
and April, to visit them that I might enjoy the first signs of their
reviving vegetation—so even now I often go and, not without a
melancholy feeling, to visit the spots where they stood and note
with pleasure that from the roots of the first two new sprouts are
shooting, and from the trunk of the third new branches are
springing which, if not healing, are to some extent hiding the
mutilation."

And here—like Cid Hamet Ben Engeli—I.F. Edler von Mosel,
composer, critic, historian, and Imperial Royal Librarian, breaks
forth into an exclamation in manner and form following, to wit:

"And a man like this who found such pure joy in the presence
of his family; who possessed such a warm feeling for the beauties
of nature; who—as we have seen—saved the life of his servant
through a truly paternal care—not a servant long proved and
faithful found, but one engaged only temporarily; who cherished
the feeling of gratitude for favors received, even to the borders
of the grave—such a man has enemies (and what extraordinary
man is free from them?) and they had the impudence to pretend
that he was guilty of the meanest and most hideous crime against
one of his brethren in art—against Mozart—and this too, on no
other ground for so shameful a slander, than not even fault-find-
ing with that great master's compositions, but only silence upon
their preeminent beauties; a silence which, even if it may have
had its origin in jealousy of the fame of a rival—of which the
noblest artist cannot fully divest himself—still could never have
been any ground for giving so deadly a thrust in his last days at
the fame of a man in every respect honorable and virtuous."

The reader has already seen that Mosel is wrong here in the
matter of Salieri's expressing his ill opinion of Mozart's dramatic
music by silence alone; but as to the rest, this burst of feeling is
creditable to him and well grounded.

But, to return to the narrative and to the year 1788.

We have seen that the year began for Salieri with the production of his amazingly popular *Axur* and that, while producing (as Kapellmeister) new works by Paisiello and Mozart during the spring, he finished the composition of Abbate Casti's *Cublai*—a heroic, comic opera.

"This opera," says Mosel, "has hitherto (1827) nowhere been given, and its performance might perhaps meet with difficulties on any stage because of its somewhat doubtful subject which is treated by the poet rather with biting satire than with good-natured wit. The music, without standing in the front rank of Salieri's works as a whole, has yet in parts much that is meritorious."

The reader may perhaps remember that in 1779, out of kindness to a composer named Rust, whom various circumstances deprived of the opportunity of bringing out the opera ordered from him for the opening of a new theater in Milan, Salieri had voluntarily given up to him the composition of the second act of *Il talismano*, and that the work proved a success. After *Cublai*, the composer turned his attention to this Milan work and wrote new music to the second act. Three new operas had been brought out under his direction [see the list given before] since *Don Giovanni*, but with so little success as to call for *Il talismano* on September 10.[2]

"The opera pleased sufficiently," says the modest composer. Truth, however, requires the expression 'very greatly,' and it fully deserved its success (Mosel). It was given nine times before the end of the year. "It is noteworthy that in this work Salieri for the first time employed clarinets and the fundamental bass plays a more important part than in most of his earlier productions. The text ranks in the better class of Italian comic operas—the number of which is not large—having the same subject with that well known drama to which Carl Maria von Weber wrote such pleasing music—*Preciosa*" (Mosel). Salieri's appointment as First Kapellmeister has been noticed. Mosel's record, confused as to dates, is as follows:

"In the same year [1788] Salieri was given the position of the

---

[2] Mosel's confusion of the dates of Salieri's labors in 1787-88 in this account have been rectified by means of the Vienna Theater Calendar and Dr. [Leopold] Sonnleithner's MS Catalogue.—A.W.T.

deceased Bonno, I.R. Kapellmeister, by which the direction of the chapel and chamber music of the court and the opera came into his hands for which the last function, however, he drew a separate salary. The chamber concerts had already begun to be less frequent and, on account of the increasing ill health of the monarch, soon ceased entirely.

"Allied with Russia, Austria took the field against the Turks. Joseph II, in spite of his feeble health, departed for the camp on February 29, 1788. To celebrate his return, Salieri prepared himself with a new Mass and a *Te Deum*; but the monarch, after his return (December 5), was almost constantly confined to his bed by the long and painful sickness which was destined to put so early an end to a life so dear to millions of men, and the *Te Deum* did not take place."

Meantime another opera, *Il pastor fido*, text by Da Ponte, was in Salieri's hands and came to performance on February 11, 1789. The text was bad and the music not remarkable—the result was nothing to boast of. *Il turco in Italia*, music by [Franz] Seidelmann, came upon the stage April 28; *I due supposti conti* and *I due baroni*, both composed by Cimarosa, respectively on May 12 and September 6; after which the first new opera was *La cifra* [December 11, 1789], of which the text was a remodeling by Da Ponte of *La dama pastorella*, composed by Salieri in Rome in 1780, and the music almost entirely new.

Da Ponte merely remarks that these two operas "formed no very brilliant point in Salieri's fame," though the latter appears to have been a success.

If, however, this year (1789), with its multiplied duties and cares and probably anxiety and grief at the condition of Joseph's health, did not add much to the composer's fame at home, he had testimonials in abundance of the spread and increase of his reputation abroad.

Mazzolà wrote him from Dresden of the immense success of *Axur* on that stage, and besought him to compose a text, *Il poeta ridicolo*, after an English piece—which, however, came to nothing.

La Salle, Secretary of the Academy of Music at Paris, offered a text, *Le Troubadour* (by an author not named), which also came to nothing. And Du Roger wrote him about a four-act text which his description shows was but a Frenchifying of Shakespeare's *Tempest.*

Matteo Liverati informed him that his *Il talismano* had been given in Potsdam in honor of the Princess of Orange.

From a pretty wide examination of the annual reports of the principal German theaters of those days, I [Thayer] draw the conclusion that in the original Italian or in German translations, the more important works of Salieri were far more popular and much oftener given than those of Mozart, while the *Grotta di Trofonio* was at least as much performed as Mozart's *Entführung.* Indeed, Paisiello's *Barbiere di Sevilla* had then a similar relation to Mozart's *Marriage of Figaro*, in regard to the frequency of performance which Rossini's *Barbiere* has in our day. In other words, with the exception of the *Entführung*, Mozart's operas were less to the taste of the monarch and the public in Vienna than those of Salieri, and it was the same way all through Germany. Whatever the appreciative few may have thought of *The Marriage of Figaro* and *Don Giovanni*, to the general operatic public Salieri was certainly the greatest of then living composers! This seems hardly possible to us in 1864, but it was so; and while it shows how little reason Salieri had to treat his rival ungenerously, it accounts satisfactorily for the bitterness of his remarks upon that rival's music, when thirty years later it was to be heard on every operatic stage, while his was forgotten!

Thus in 1789, Salieri, in his fortieth year, had attained all the objects to which a musician could look as the aims of his ambition. He was Imperial Royal Kapellmeister of the Emperor of Germany [*sic*]; his combined salaries made him comparatively rich; his successes at Paris gave him not only fame but a steady income from the Grand Opera; his works were given everywhere and were considered standard pieces; from all sides came orders for new works, the then most distinguished operatic poets wishing to have their texts put into his hands; he was already the great teacher of operatic composition and, but a few years later, numbered Beethoven among his pupils.

CHAPTER 9

The Deaths of Joseph II and Mozart; Salieri's Political Decline

FROM THE POINT WHICH is now reached in the life of Salieri, Mosel hurries on to the conclusion, epitomizing the rest into a very small space. I shall follow his example, not from a lack of matter, but because I cannot suppose others to feel my interest in the history, and because there must be somewhere a limit to an article prepared for a journal.[1] From what has been already detailed, the reader must see that at this period, 1790, Salieri stood at the head of the living musical operatic composers of the world in popular estimation. The greatness of Mozart's works was known to an "appreciative few," and those works were establishing themselves in their true position; but they were—*Die Entführung aus dem Serail* excepted—on the whole, caviar to the generality, and the *Magic Flute,* which was the magic wand to open the popular ear to his exquisite melodies and divine harmonies, was not yet composed. Salieri, therefore, stood before the world in 1790, as Rossini did in 1830, the acknowledged greatest living composer for the stage.

The year 1790 began with a heavy blow both to Salieri and Mozart—Joseph II died on the 20th of February. His successor was his brother, the narrow-minded, bigoted, despotic Leopold II, Grand Duke of Tuscany. It takes long to mature, adopt, and put in force any great measure of state; but the repeal of a law, the return to the old way, the re-adoption of the old policy is the work of a moment. This Leopold proved anew. The

---

[1] Thayer's biography of Salieri was, of course, serialized in twenty-three issues of *Dwight's Journal of Music* in 1863-64.—T.A.

measures and general polity which Joseph, by many years of labor and perseverance, had but fairly introduced and which were intended to make Austria an enlightenend and progressive state—which curbed the insolence of its greedy, immoral, and debased priesthood, reducing in number and power its everywhere swarming legions of monks, which encouraged freedom of thought and speech, improved the schools, and was building up domestic industry in all directions—these measures, this polity were annihilated by a stroke of the pen. The man seems to have adopted as his rule of action, the maxim that whatever had pleased Joseph must for that reason be detested by Leopold. This was as true in relation to the theater and music as to politics and public affairs. On March 13, he assumed the crown—on July 15, a writer records: "The present king has not yet been in a theater, has had no music at home, nor has given any sign of love for music." These facts, however, the writer supposes to be owing to the pressure of public business, and that "the golden age of music would begin a new epoch, after the giant mountains of state affairs had been reduced to sand hills." Since Leopold died on March 1, 1792, there proved to be hardly time for the new musical epoch to open.

The accession of Leopold, however, does not seem to have had any immediate effect upon the position of Salieri, although of course, after the death of Joseph, the court theaters were closed for a time, and the Kapellmeister was for so long relieved of his duties in the orchestra.

His first work of this year, 1790, appears to have been the changes made in *Tarare* for the Opera in Paris. Towards the end of the preceding year, this popular work had been neglected, the leading parts given to inferior actors and singers, and finally, it was withdrawn altogether to the great loss of the treasury and the great wrath of Beaumarchais. By February 1790, the directors began sensibly to feel the mistake, and a deputation from them waited upon the poet and, after admitting that the receipts of the opera house had fallen below the necessary expenses, prayed him to bring *Tarare* again upon the stage. They desired, however, that the piece should close with a magnificent spectacle, the Coronation of Tarare, promising to employ only singers and dancers of the very first class in it. Beaumarchais at last consented to make the necessary alterations which consisted in the addition of the new finale, and a consequent shortening of the previous acts. Impatient to draw the pecuniary benefits of the revival, the directors applied to Le Moine and Grétry to compose the new music and thus save them from the loss of time involved in sending for it to Vienna. Whatever may have been the motive—pride, modesty, or consideration for Salieri—the French composers refused the engagement, and Beaumarchais forced the committee to make formal application to his friend by letter. He sent a letter, with his texts to the Coronation scene and to certain other pieces which were to be introduced, in which he told Salieri: "You will certainly find it [the Coronation] in importance adequate to the position [as a new finale to the very successful *Tarare*]. With the election of a beloved king by a liberated people, I have associated several of the grand questions with which the nation is just now busied."

These questions were, says Mosel, the marriage of ecclesiastics, the cancelling of marriages (which was brought into the piece by the divorce of the two characters, Calpigi and Spinette) and other such productions of that unhappy epoch. A letter from the Committee of June 2, 1790, and another from Beaumarchais of the 6th, urged Salieri to hasten his work and visit Paris to superintend its production as well as bring out his new work *Castor and Pollux*, a text, however, which he did not compose. Salieri was detained in Vienna and sent his new music to the Committee. In the middle of August, Beaumarchais announced the extraordinary success of the opera in its new form.

"It was put upon the stage with astonishing pains," he said, "and enjoyed by the public as a sublime work of the musical art. You now rank with us, at the head of all composers! The treasury of the opera, which for a year past has received by 500 or 600 livres a night, made with *Tarare* 6540 livres at the first performance and 5400 at the second. The performers who have this time carefully observed my maxim to consider their singing as but a supplement to the action have, for the first time, been ranked among the greatest actors of the stage, and the public cried; 'That is music—not a single fantastic note! Everything is aimed at the grand effect of the dramatic action.' What a pleasure for me, my friend, to see justice thus done you and to hear you unanimously called the worthy successor of Gluck." In a later letter Beaumarchais wrote: "I repeat to you that the French public feels the dramatic beauties of the music in *Tarare* more than ever. This is the only work that gives the Opera a profit."

Mosel is of the opinion that Salieri's disgust at the principles advocated in the Coronation of Tarare was the reason why he did not go to Paris to bring it out—a view which finds some confirmation in the fact that no copy of it was found, after the composer's death, among his music. But Salieri had other duties at this time. As chief Kapellmeister, it devolved upon him to prepare and conduct the music at the various coronations of [Emperor] Leopold. One of the compositions composed expressly for these occasions was a grand *Te Deum.* The ceremony at Prague where Leopold was crowned King of Bohemia took place on September 6; his election as Emperor of Germany followed on the 30th of the same month at Frankfurt a. M., and the coronation on the 6th of October; his coronation as King of Hungary, at Pressburg, took place on November 15. In the list of Leopold's suite at Frankfurt, as given in the *Kronungs-Diarium* (2 vols., folio), we read:

K. K. Hofkapelle (Imp. Roy. Court Chapel).

Herr Anton Salieri, I. R. Court Kapellmeister.

Herr Ignaz Umlauf, *substitut* [Deputy Kapellmeister].

15 Chamber musicians.

In 1791, Salieri petitioned to be relieved of the direction of the Italian Opera with which, except during his absences in Paris and Italy, he had been charged now for four and twenty years. His prayer was granted with the condition that he should still have charge of the sacred music in the palace chapel, and should deliver an opera annually to the stage. Joseph Weigl, a pupil of Salieri, took his place in the opera, being appointed to that place by Leopold as he himself said, "to honor the master through his scholar." Mosel makes the resignation of Salieri a transaction creditable to Leopold's goodness of heart, but other authorities give quite a different view of the matter. Leopold's mind was thoroughly poisoned against the managers of the imperial theater; moreover, he intended, instead of the German Opera and the Italian Opera Buffa, to establish the Opera Seria and Ballet on a grand scale and to put up a new house for them. Hence we read among the various remarks made by Leopold in the conversation recorded by Da Ponte [in his *Memoirs*], which bear upon the first point the following:

Da Ponte: "Salieri, too. ..."

Leopold: "It is unnecessary for you to speak of Salieri. I know him sufficiently. I know all his cabals and those also of Cavalieri [a prima donna of the Opera Buffa].[2] He is an intolerable egotist, and would like to have nothing succeed in my theater but his operas and his favorites; he is not only your enemy, but that of all the Kapellmeisters, all the singers, all the Italians, and especially mine, because he knows that I see through him. I will not longer have either his German woman [Catarina Cavalieri was, in fact, born in Vienna] or himself in my theater."

The Berlin *Musikalisches Wochenblatt* records in October, 1791:

> It is said that Salieri has resigned, and that [Domenico] Cimarosa has been called to his position. . . . As to the intentions of the former, nothing is yet distinctly known, but it is believed that he will establish his residence in Paris, where he has already produced three operas, in consequence of which he receives a handsome pension. Some are of the opinion that the cause of his dissatisfaction lies in the proposed plan of a new court theater in which the boxes are to be fitted up for card playing.

Again:

> Vienna, October 20 [1791]. Kapellmeister Salieri has retired, retaining his full salary, but will for the future furnish an operetta annually to the Italian stage.

To which the editor (Johann Friedrich Reichardt) remarks in a note:

> We desire to have from some competent Viennese, the particulars in relation to this piece of news. Why is so young and excellent a composer put upon the retired list? Has a special troupe for the grand Court Opera been engaged? And is this company paid so much less than the Opera Buffa formerly was, one

---

[2] And reputedly Salieri's mistress, although the puritanical Thayer would not have thought it proper to mention that fact as well in clarification of Leopold's contemptuous reference. The reference to "his German woman" following was, in fact, given by Thayer as "his Germans," which renders the passage into nonsense.—T.A.

member of which, the songstress [Nancy] Storace for instance, received 1000 ducats annually?

But the changes made by Leopold were general. Count [Orsini] Rosenberg, the director, gave way to Count [Johann Wenzel] Ugarte; Da Ponte, the poet, and [Adriana] Ferrarese, prima donna, dismissed in disgrace, etc. At all events Salieri's forty-first birthday (August 19 [actually the 18th]) saw him on the point of leaving that orchestra forever in which he so long had labored. With his departure the orchestra began to lose its excellence. In less than ten years a writer in the Leipzig *Allgemeine musikalische Zeitung* (June 10, 1801) could say:

> When the worthy Salieri was Kapellmeister of the Italian Opera, and Herr Scheidlein, if I am not mistaken, was director of the orchestra, the members were the same as now (a few excepted who may have left it), and yet the operas were executed so that the severest criticism could demand nothing more. The perfect time of all the instruments and the precision with which all worked together were among the least of its excellencies. The voices were accompanied with extreme delicacy; every shade, to the very lightest, in the accompaniments brought out; the exact expression always hit. At that time this orchestra was indisputably one of the very first theater orchestras in Germany, a fact admitted by every competent judge. But when Salieri had to give up his position to another, and Herr [Jacopo] Conti became leader, the orchestra sank by degrees until it fell to the point where it now stands. The fault must therefore lie not in its members, but rather in its leaders.

During this year (1791), when Mozart, discouraged and disheartened in his career as operatic composer, sought the appointment of successor to [Leopold] Hofmann as Kapellmeister in St. Stephan's church [*Stephansdom*] and gladly accepted the order of the buffoon Schikaneder to compose *The Magic Flute*, and of the authorities at Prague to compose *La clemenza di Tito*, which two works he just lived to complete with young [Franz Xaver] Süssmayr's aid. Salieri, though politely disgraced by his Emperor and set aside, was receiving orders for operas from vari-

ous quarters. Beaumarchais and the directors of the Grand
Opera still continued to urge him to come to Paris and a new
text, *La Princesse de Babylone* by [Désiré] Martin, was put into his
hands. The turn which the Revolution took there, however, prevented the composer from accepting the invitation. Mazzolà, the
poet at Dresden, promised very soon to make such changes in
his text, *L' isola capricciosa,* as the composer desired, offered him
again *Il poeta ridicolo,* and informed him that *Axur* had met with
such a success in Dresden, "that every other opera, however
beautiful, seemed weak when compared with this." Still another
text was sent him from Padua, *Alessio,* by [Antonio Simone]
Sografi, of which, however, nothing came.

At one o'clock on the night of December 4-5, 1791, Mozart
died. At 3 p.m. on the 6th, the funeral ceremony took place in
the Cross Chapel in the North transept of St. Stephan's. Salieri
was one of the few who were present in spite of a terrible storm
with rain and sleet. Whether he was one of those who went with
the remains to the city gate but there turned back appalled by
the rage of the storm sweeping across the broad open glacis,
does not appear.[3] Seventeen years later (1808) appeared the second edition of [Franz Xaver] Niemetschek's short biography of
Mozart in which (p. 81) the following anecdote is given:

> A still living and not undistinguished composer in
> Vienna [Salieri is said to be meant, remarks Jahn] said
> to another, when Mozart died, with much truth and jus-
> tice: "It is indeed sad, the loss of so great a genius; but
> well for us that he is dead. For had he lived longer, veri-
> ly, the world would not have given us another bit of
> bread for our compositions!"

Whether the anecdote be authentic, especially whether Salieri
really is meant, certainly admits of doubt. But as years went on
and the Italian saw the works of his rival growing in the public
estimation until they were put by the whole musical world at the
head of all operas and their influence was felt in all schools of
operatic composition; when he saw *Don Giovanni* and *The Marriage of Figaro* everywhere on the stage while his own works, which
had so surpassed them in immediate success, had become par-

---

[3] Recent research indicates no storm on the day of Mozart's funeral; rather, mild weather. Nicolas Slonimsky, "The Weather at Mozart's Funeral," *Musical Quarterly* 46 (1960), 12-21.—T.A.

tially forgotten, it is true a feeling of bitterness grew up in the heart of the older man which, in private circles during his last years, found vent in words.

On Thursday, March 1, 1792, Emperor Leopold followed his brother Joseph "to the other side" (*jenseits,* as the Germans express it) after an illness of only thirty-six hours. At the coronation of his successor, Franz I, as King of Bohemia and as Emperor of Germany—the latter at Frankfurt on July 14—Salieri again had the direction of the music which consisted mainly of the same pieces which had been performed on similar occasions two years before.

Changes in the direction of the opera, as well as other causes occurred, which in succeeding years relieved Salieri from his duty of delivering an annual composition for the stage. Still the number of his works was largely increased. I shall content myself, and doubtless more than content most readers, by simply adding a chronological list of these works. The little that remains to be said of the quiet life, which for another thirty-three years the composer led, mostly in Vienna, can then close the narrative.

1791. *Catilina,* 2 acts, text by Abbate Casti, never performed. It was a tragi-comic work in which the chief comic character was Marcus Tullius Cicero! One Italian wrote, another composed it; of course it was all right.

Salieri seems also in this year to have composed a part of [Désiré] Martin's *Princesse de Babylone,* and to have gone on with the next work noted, viz:

1793. *Il mondo alla rovescia,* which he had formerly begun for Venice, under the title *L'isola capricciosa,* 2 acts, brought out under the direction of Baron [Peter] von Braun on January 13, 1795. In this text men have the duties, cares, characters and feelings of women and vice versa. The men are the blushing and modest objects of the stormy passion of the other sex. It proved a bad subject for the stage and a failure.

1794. *Eraclito e Democrito,* text by Gamerra, 2 acts. Salieri calls this in his own papers, "Operetta buffa filosofica," a very good descriptive title for a work which presents the weeping and laughing philosophers. It was produced on August 13, and had a fair run until superseded by:

Palmira, "opera eroica comica" in 2 acts, text by Gamerra, drawn from the *Le Princesse de Babylone*, sent to Salieri from Paris, as already noted. None of the music which he had composed to the French text was retained to the Italian words, for the same reasons which had led him to compose *Axur* anew when Joseph II wished for *Tarare*. Premiered on October 14, 1795, this was one of the master's most successful and famous works and in 1803 was reproduced in the Theater an der Wien, revised and with alterations by him. It not only made the rounds of the German stage in Italian or in German translation but, in 1812, was brought out at Warsaw in the Polish language. In this opera appears for the first time, so far as I know or at least recollect, a vocal unaccompanied quartet, "Silenzio facciasi," an effect made common enough since but then a new and striking proof of the simple means by which true genius produces great effects. This was invariably repeated.

1796. For the annual concerts for the benefit of the widows and orphans of Vienna musicians, established by Gassmann in 1771, and especially to celebrate the twenty-fifth anniversary of the Association [*Tonkünstler-Sozietät*], Salieri composed a cantata entitled *La riconoscenza*, consisting of a chorus, recitative and aria with concerted instruments. The vocalist was the composer's pupil, Gassmann's second daughter, Theresa. Salieri had taught her ten years gratis and had made her one of the ornaments of the Vienna stage. Not expecting, with his feeble frame, to live to see the fiftieth anniversary of the Society, Salieri wrote at the end of the score:

> The author of this Cantata sends greeting and peace from the lap of eternity to that composer who shall write the Thanksgiving Cantata for the celebration of the half century, and to all who shall assist in the performances.
>
> Vienna, 1796   Salieri.

His opera this year was *Il moro*, opera buffa, 2 acts, text by Gamerra, performed on August 7. It had some excellent numbers, but was no success. Orgone, the lover of the piece, sings always in falsetto and is asked by the Moor why that is. Orgone replies:

> ... Ella sappia
Che si danno fra noi certi spettacoli

Chiamati opere serie, e che son veri
Mostri dell' arte. In esse
Fur sempre i maschi amanti,
Che dicon mille e mille cose tenere,
Per legge teatral di neutro genere.

(You must know that with us there is a kind of play
called *Opere Serie,* which are true monsters of Art. In
these it has always been the rule to have the lovers, who
say thousands upon thousands of tender things, of the
neuter gender.)

So Orgone must sing falsetto in order to make love like the
eunuchs [*castrati*] who performed the heroes in Handel's and all
the other Italian operas of his time and for many years after. A
satire that hits also such parts as the lover in Rossini's *Romeo and
Juliet,* sung by women [*sic*].

1797. *I tre filosofi,* also by Gamerra, in which the systems of
Pirro, Diogenes and Pythagoras appear in ludicrous contest,
remained a fragment.

Falstaff, ossia Le tre burle, opera buffa, in 2 acts, text by
Defranceschi. First performance January 2, 1799. Of course the
subject is [Shakespeare's] *Merry Wives of Windsor.* The overture is
lively English contre-dance music, the cue being taken from the
first words of the introduction: "Poi si torni di nuovo a ballar!"
("Then begin the dance anew!"). In the opening scene Bardolph
sits talking in his sleep, in a low monotone until the last note,
which is very high and loud; for Falstaff enters and gives him a
punch in the ribs at that point to wake him. It is curious that one
of the arias is in German—sung by Mistress Ford ["O, die Män-
ner kenn' ich schon"] ("Ah, the men—I know them well!"). No.
3 is a duet: "La stessa la stessissima."[4] Ten variations upon it by
Ludwig van Beethoven [WoO 73] are advertised in the *Wiener
Zeitung* of March 2, two months after the first performance of the
opera.

A still greater compliment from the same source was paid him
a few months later. That proud, impetuous young genius, moving in the higher circle of Viennese society among princes and
counts of the empire, as an equal with equals, the dedications of

---

[4] Thayer provides the theme's incipit in musical notation, not reproduced here, but easily
found in the Kinsky-Halm catalogue of Beethoven's works.—T.A.

whose works thus far—except a few minor importance and the Sonatas [Op. 2] dedicated to Haydn—had been to kings, princes and persons of noble birth, published his Opus 12 with the following title: "Tre Sonate per il clavicembalo o Forte-Piano, con un Violino, Composte e dedicate al Sig^r Antonio Salieri, prima Maestro di capella della Corte Imperiale di Vienna, &c., &c., dal Sig^r Luigi van Beethoven, Opera 12. A Vienna, Presso Artaria e Comp." Beethoven had been studying dramatic composition with Salieri, and this dedication was a pure mark of esteem and gratitude—it was really a compliment.

1799. Two cantatas: *Der Tiroler Landsturm*, in German, and *La riconoscenza dei Tirolesi*, in Italian, composed for the benefit of the suffering Tyrolese and performed at a grand concert in Vienna, belong to this year; as also a Mass, with *Graduale, Offertorium* and *Te Deum*, all in double chorus, intended for performance on occasion of the declaration of peace with the French republic; but as the peace was not concluded, the music was for the time laid aside.

1800. *Cesare in Farmacusa*, opera eroi-comica, 2 acts, text by [Carlo Prospero] Defranceschi, was on produced on June 2, successfully. Among Salieri's own notes upon this work is one which Mosel cites. There is a bass aria in the first act in which Tullo laments the danger of starving. "The aria is comic," writes the composer, "for the reason that when the comic actor weeps upon the stage, the audience must laugh."

Angiolina, ossia Il matrimonio per sussuro, opera buffa, 2 acts, text by [Carlo Prospero] Defranceschi, produced on October 22, had some success through the excellent music, though the text was almost beneath criticism.

1801. *Annibale in Capua*, opera seria, 2 acts, text by advocate [Antonio Simone] Sografi, composed at and for the opening of the new theater in Trieste. It was successful there, but nowhere else does it appear to have been put upon the stage and for a very good reason: Salieri had, of course, to accommodate his music to the powers of his singers, and the leading character was written for a *castrato*, as in olden times was so common. Think of the mighty Hannibal, quavering and roulading in soprano!

From Trieste the composer was to have gone on to Venice; but the prospect of peace and the wish to conduct his double choruses at the celebration of it at home was stronger than his desire to earn money or laurels by so everyday a matter as composing an opera. On arriving in Vienna he found a new invitation to Paris awaiting him, with the first act of a text (*Les Troyennes*, by R. Bernard); but this he also declined.

1802. *La bella selvaggia*, opera in 2 acts, text by [Giovanni] Bertati, not brought out. The subject was not that of [Paul Wranitzky's] ballet *Das Waldmädchen* (Girl of the Forest), a theme from which was varied by Beethoven [WoO 71], and of the opera by Weber, but rather concerns a wild girl supposed to be found by the Spaniards on an American island.

Die Neger (The Negroes), a heroic-comic German opera, 2 acts, text by Friedrich Treitschke, composed in 1802, but first given in the Theater an der Wien, November 10, 1804, on the stage where one year later Beethoven's *Fidelio* met such ill success.

Cantata for Archduke Ferdinand, prepared in anticipation of the delivery of the archduchess. As both mother and child died (September 19, 1802), of course the piece was not performed.

1803. Overture, entr'actes and choruses to [August von] Kotzebue's *The Hussites before Naumburg* [*Die Hussiten vor Naumburg*], a noble work of the stamp of Beethoven's *Egmont* music.

Gesù al limbo, sacred cantata, text by [Luigi?] Prividali, composed for the Empress, and sung at the palace. The overture—or rather symphony [*sinfonia*]—was a piece of programme music which, for its ludicrous want of intelligibility unless heard with a running commentary before the eyes, would do honor to any of the great lights of the so-called "new school" composers [Liszt and Wagner?—T.A.]. This piece of music was intended to depict the entire life of Jesus in tones. Accordingly in Salieri's score may be read, often to passages of not more than four to eight bars of music, such notes as these: "Gesù in mezzo ai dottori" (Jesus in the midst of the doctors), "Arrestamento di Gesù" (Arrest of Jesus), "Viene interrogato" (his examination), etc.

1804. *Requiem Mass*, composed for performance at his own funeral obsequies, whenever they might take place.

On December 8, Salieri had the satisfaction of conducting the Mass for double chorus, composed five years before. It was given upon occasion of the celebration of the adoption by Franz I of the title of Emperor of Austria.

1805. *Habsburg* [cantata]. This was a long poem of a historic-allegoric character, with no variety of rhythm, and merely divided into stanzas not intended for music but as an offering to the new Emperor of Austria. The author, Ferdinand [Freiherr] von Geramb it seems, formed the plan of arranging a national festival the next year at which his poem should be sung as a cantata. But hardly was the music ready when the question came up whether an Austrian nation was to exist. On October 17, Ulm capitulated to the French army; on the 30th, Bernadotte entered Salzburg; and on November 16, Murat marched into Vienna. Beethoven's *Fidelio* was given to an audience mainly of French—but Salieri's Cantata in praise of the Habsburgs, it is hardly necessary to add, was laid upon the shelf. It was, of course, no loss to the musical world.

Another Mass and church pieces suited to the times—a *Miserere*, a *De profundis*, a *Salvum fac populum*, etc., employed Salieri's pen during the last half of this year.

At this point [p. 171], Mosel gives a summary of Salieri's other compositions down to this time. They were: an organ concerto, 1775; two pianoforte concertos, 1778; a concerto for violin, oboe and violoncello, 1774; a symphony, 1776; five serenatas for various instruments; 40 canons for three voices—"all written," says Salieri, "during my walks or when in the company of musicians or amateurs, who could sing them on the spot"—more than a hundred vocal pieces for church, theater or the private circle; twenty-eight vocal pieces with pianoforte accompaniment, and various smaller matters. A collection containing twenty-five of those canons (*a tre voci*) and a trio was published in 1815, with the title *Scherzi armonici vocali.*

CHAPTER 10

Salieri's Final Two Decades, Physical and Mental Decline, and Death

F ROM THIS POINT DOWN TO 1816 there is a break in Salieri's account of his own history as composer—a period of eleven years—and one which Mosel only partially fills with notices drawn mainly from the correspondence found among Salieri's papers. From these notices and from other sources, let a slight picture of this portion of his life be drawn—from his 56th to his 66th year. It was the period of the Napoleonic wars, one of domestic calamity and sorrow to the composer, from whom his son, three of his daughters, and, at last, his angel of a wife were taken. [Theresia Helferstorfer Salieri died on August 30, 1807.] Moreover, the change in public taste in relation to the opera was one which to him seemed all for the worse. Of this change he writes:

> From that period I became aware that the taste for that [dramatic] music was turning gradually into a direction quite contrary to that of my time. Extravagance and a confusion of the various species of composition introduced themselves in the place of a rational and masterly simplicity.[1]

Altogether, it is not at all remarkable that he rejected even the two applications which came to him from the Parisian Grand Opera in these years, to compose for the stage. He obeyed an

---

[1] Da quell' epoca poi mi sono ancora accorto che il gusto della musica si andava a poco la volta cangiando in una maniera tutto affatto contraria a'miei tempi. La stravaganza e la confusione dei generi si è introdotta in luogo d'una ragionata e maestrale semplicita.—A.W.T.

order from the Vienna Opera which had now become permanently German—the visits of Italian troupes being already but extra seasons—to revise and alter the second act of his famous French work *Les Danaïdes*, with a German text by Franz Xaver Huber (author of the words to Beethoven's *Christ on the Mount of Olives*), but circumstances prevented it from coming to performance. Besides this, I find that during this time no mention of any dramatic work from his pen—that pen which from 1769 (*Le donne letterate*) to 1802 (*Die Neger*) had given to the stage thirty-nine complete operas, and which had made him known from Naples to Riga, from Paris to Warsaw.

But that pen was by no means inactive, though in another field. The number of his compositions for the church—that is, for special use in the palace chapel—was greatly increased; such as a Vesper service consisting of six psalms, a hymn, a *Salve Regina* and a litany; a number of Graduales, Offertoires and the like. He wrote five patriotic choruses, four of which came to performance on public occasions during the wars—for instance, one with an echo: "May Providence, oh happy Austria, protect thee," which closed a concert opened by Beethoven's *Coriolan* overture, on April 25, 1814; and in 1816 he published twenty-four variations for full orchestra upon a theme called "La Folia di Spagna."

During these years the master's ordinary course of life was generally this: four days in the week the morning hours were taken up with his duties in the chapel and as Vice-president of the Institute for Musicians' Widows and Orphans [*Witwen- und Pensions-Institut der Tonkünstler*]. On the other three days, the hours from nine to one were devoted to giving instruction, *gratis*, in singing, thorough bass and composition to students of both sexes. His afternoons were spent in his long walks; his evenings with musical friends where the works of Gluck, of the old Italian masters and such of his own as were unknown in Vienna, or had long been laid aside, formed the staple of the evening's entertainment. He was a voracious reader, and what time remained over was devoted to books. He had much literary taste and most, if not all, the texts to his *Scherzi armonici* were of his own authorship. He very seldom visited the theater, and the more so as composers departed more widely from what he held to be the only true dramatic style. He believed that a reaction would take place, and that a time would come when simplicity and delicacy of expression would again be the aim of the dramatic composer.

That time has not yet (1864) come; but the enormous demand for new editions of Mozart's, Haydn's, and other composers' works for the pianoforte, shows a reaction from the monstrosities of the pseudo new school [i.e., Liszt and Wagner—T.A.] in that branch of music, as the revival of Handel and Bach, and the study of their works in their completeness does in another; and one can but hope that by and by the braying of brass and the crash of barbaric noise-making tools will give place in the operatic orchestra to—music.

The gloom caused by Salieri's domestic sorrow, however, seems to have been brightened by his religious faith; as any feelings of disappointment which the course of public taste had taken, in Vienna at least, were consoled by the evidence of esteem and regard which came to him from all quarters, and by revivals of some of his works, made with splendid success.

At the celebrated production of *The Creation* on March 27, 1808, at which Haydn was present for the last time, when all that

Performance of Haydn's Creation on March 27, 1808 (detail). Haydn sits in the place of honor; Beethoven, with cane in hand, stands to his left; Salieri, who conducted, stands behind Haydn with roll of paper in his hand.

was distinguished in the musical world of Vienna came together to do the old man honor, and women of the highest ranks of the nobility gave their shawls to protect him from the draft, it was Salieri who held the chief place—who conducted. In December 1813, Salieri joined in those two grand concerts in which Beethoven produced his Seventh Symphony and his *Wellington's Victory, or The Battle of Vittoria,* not thinking it beneath his dignity to conduct the band of drums and clashing instruments which represent the shock of the contending armies.

One great enjoyment during those years was afforded him by the Moravian Count Heinrich von Haugwitz. This nobleman, a devout admirer of the solid compositions of Gluck, [Johann Gottlieb] Naumann, and especially Handel, and wealthy enough to retain his own orchestra and singers, not only called Salieri in to conduct the works of those composers when in Vienna but, during several summers, had him at his seat in Moravia. There Salieri's two passions were gratified to the full, his love for Gluck and Handel, and his love of nature.

In the spring of 1813, there came letters to him from Paris which did his heart good; they announced the performance there of his *Axur* at the Italian Opera with a success amounting to enthusiasm—not less than that which this opera in its original form, as *Tarare,* had won on the French stage. After the aria of Aspasia, "Son queste le speranze," the clapping of hands, shouting "Viva Salieri!" lasted nearly a quarter of an hour.

The foundation at Vienna of the great Society of the Friends of Music [Gesellschaft der Musikfreunde] about this time [1812] gave him another opportunity to labor for the cause of good music, which he embraced and for some time led the weekly rehearsals. For this Society he composed a very curious work, a *Scuola di canto* (School of Singing), in which all the rules are versified and then the stanzas set to such music as illustrates the very words which one is singing.

Another work of this period was a *Libro di partimenti di varia specie,* a plan for private study and instruction in the nine species of musical composition, which comprehended a full explanation of the characteristics of each. As a further illustration, he prepared the skeleton of an opera in which could be introduced any desirable examples of these species of composition, the person portraying a Kapellmeister explaining their peculiarities. Salieri supposed, too, that such an opera might be the medium for bringing upon the stage many works or parts of works of deserving but forgotten composers. One stubborn fact, however, stands in the way of such a project: people go to the opera for amusement, not for instruction.

The reader may perhaps remember that Gassmann reached Vienna with the boy Antonio Salieri on June 15, 1766, and that the first thing the next morning was to take him to the Italian church to perform his devotions; and that on the way home the master said to his pupil: "I thought I must begin your musical education with God. It will now depend upon yourself whether the result shall be good or bad. At all events I shall have done my duty!"

The 16th of June, 1816, the semi-centennial anniversary of that first walk in Vienna, was coming on apace, and was longingly anticipated both by Salieri and his friends. They had determined to celebrate it in a becoming manner; but more than all—and so far as appears, quite unknown to the composer—Emperor Franz I was preparing a surprise for him. Early on the morning of that day, Salieri, accompanied by the four daughters who remained to him, went to the Italian church to offer his thanks to the Almighty for all the blessings and the extraordinary success which had crowned his fifty years of conscientious study and labor. At ten in the morning, a court carriage took him to the hotel of Prince Trautmannsdorf-Weinberg, chief marshal at court, where he found all the members of the chapel awaiting him in the anteroom. The prince and Count [Johann Ferdinand] Kueffstein, the *Hofmusikgraf* (general director of the Court music), immediately entered and led him into the room selected for the little ceremony which was coming. The members of the chapel came in and arranged themselves in a half circle in the front of which Trautmannsdorf and Kueffstein took their places with Salieri between them. The former now made an address to the composer, explaining in the most flattering terms, the grounds upon which the Emperor had decided to decorate him with the great civic gold medal and chain of honor. At the close of the address, the Prince hung the chain about his neck and embraced him; Kueffstein then followed with a short speech and embrace. Salieri's reply, out of a full heart, was a simple expression of thanks, with the remark in substance that his soul at this joyful moment was filled with double delight from the proof afforded him of the monarch's satisfaction with his efforts, and because he had the opportunity here to express his sincere thanks to his fellow-servants of the chapel, for their unremitting zeal in sustaining him, and in gaining the chapel its widespread fame. After a few minutes spent in receiving the congratulations of the gentlemen present, he drove to the palace chapel—it being Sunday—to conduct the usual eleven o'clock grand mass. He chose one of his own masses for performance with gradual and offertory, also by him, in which both text and music expressed praise and thanks to the Most High.

After service came a dinner in the company of his four daughters and a few intimate friends. Towards six o'clock, in answer to special invitations, his past and present pupils—except Johann Nepomuk Hummel and Ignaz Moscheles, who were not then in Vienna—assembled: Carl von Doblhof, Joseph Weigl, Ignaz Joseph Stuntz, Franz Schubert, Assmayer, Liszt (not the pianist),[2] students of composition; Mozatti, Fröhlich, Platzer and Salzmann, singers; Madams Maria Theresa Rosenbaum[3] and Maria Anna Fux—both were daughters of his old teacher Gassmann —and twelve others of his female pupils in singing.

Salieri placed himself at the piano-forte with his daughters beside him, all dressed alike; at his right hand the fourteen female pupils in a half circle; at his left the twelve men similarly placed. In front two seats had been placed for Trautmannsdorf and Kueffstein—the former, however, happened to be called out to Schönbrunn by the arrival of the Emperor from Italy—the latter was present. Between the seats placed for these noblemen,

[2] Mosel, p. 184, lists "Liszt" among those present, although the future virtuoso/composer was less than five years old in June 1816, and in fact, would not begin his studies with Salieri until mid-July 1822. It is not clear whom Thayer had in mind in his parenthetical qualification, possibly Anton Liste, a German who had studied with Mozart and Albrechtsberger, although he seems to have been back in central Germany by 1804.—T.A.

[3] Maria Theresa's husband kept an extensive diary from 1797 until his death in 1829; it has long been regarded as one of the most important source documents for the history of Vienna during this eventful period. Rosenbaum is perhaps most infamously remembered as the person who engineered the theft of Haydn's head after his funeral. The musical and cultural events recorded by Rosenbaum from 1797 to 1809 are given in "The Diaries of Joseph Carl Rosenbaum, 1770-1829," translated by Eugene Hartzell, edited by Else Radant, *Haydn Yearbook* 5 (1968), entire volume, 158 pp.— T.A.

stood a bust of Joseph II, his first master "and, I may say," adds Salieri in his notes, "my father, protector, and benefactor." When all were in their places, the Kapellmeister made a short speech in his usual broken German ("How can I have thoroughly learned German, since I have only lived fifty years in Germany?" he was in the habit of saying when jesting upon his incapacity to bring his Italian organs to the correct enunciation of the German gutturals)—praying his friends and pupils to thank God, in his name, for His mercy, in granting him a life now of fifty years in Vienna and in the service of the Imperial Court, "at least without disgrace to his native land, his family and his friends." This thanksgiving consisted on the part of the pupils in singing a chorus of which both words and music were by Salieri. Then followed pieces suited to the occasion by each of his pupils in composition, beginning with the most recent of them, and including two which had been sent in by the absent Hummel and Moscheles. The concert closed by singing some numbers of one of Salieri's oratorios, consisting of solos, choruses, and an echo from the next room.

On the same day, he received the imperial permission to accept his diploma as member of the French Academy, and the medal of the Legion of Honor sent him by Louis XVIII, both granted in acknowledgment of his distinguished services in the cause of music and of the great reputation gained by his works for the Parisian stage. What, doubtless, added much to the interest of this occasion was the fact that the year before, Salieri had been brought very low by a fit of sickness.

A revival at Paris, in 1817, with immense success of *Les Danaïdes,* with a very few slight changes in the music and some new dances composed by Gasparo Spontini, Ferdinando Paër and Henri-Montan Berton, brought Salieri not only an increase of income, but exceedingly grateful letters from Spontini, Pierre Louis Moline, Louis-Luc Loiseau Persuis (Director of the Grand Opera), and Hérold, composer of *Zampa.* The latter says:

> All Paris will hear this beautiful opera, and the vast crowds which besiege the doors of the theater at each performance, prove that we know how to appreciate your works. One thing we heartily lament—that we cannot see you here in Paris. Happy they who, like me, can

listen to you and benefit by your instructions. How much I regret that I did not remain longer in Vienna. I shall never forget what you have done for me, and least of all the kindness with which you gave me many an excellent piece of advice. The good fortune which I have thus far had upon the stage I attribute entirely to the instruction which I had from you—your teachings are invaluable.

Salieri's duties in the chapel during the year 1818 were relieved by preparing his *Tarare* for a new revival at the Paris Grand Opera; by some small works for the Gesellschaft der Musikfreunde and their Conservatorium [founded in 1817]; and by an excursion with Count Moritz Dietrichstein, and as his guest, to the various seats of that nobleman. *Tarare* came to the stage again on February 3, 1819, and in August, Persuis sent Salieri 1100 francs as his percentage on the profits of the two revised operas.

I find nothing noted as belonging to this year (1819), except the finishing of a grand *Te Deum*, though Mosel says he passed the summer in the country and employed himself "in select society, with singing, reading, and the composition of new or the improving of old works."

In the spring of 1820 he began a labor which was purely one of gratitude and love.

The Pension-Institute for the Widows and Orphans of Vienna Musicians [*Pensions-Institut für Witwen und Wiesen der Wiener Tonkünstler*] was founded by Gassmann and incorporated by the imperial government in 1771; the act granting not only a handsome sum of money down, but the right to give four benefit concerts annually—two at Christmas and two in Holy Week—on days when no theaters were allowed to be opened for the usual performances. For the first of these concerts (1771), Gassmann composed Metastasio's oratorio libretto *Betulia liberata*, which was brought out with upwards of two hundred performers—at that time a large number.

Salieri's composition for the twenty-fifth anniversary of that institution in 1796 has been already noticed. From that time he had always taken part in the concerts; for some he delivered new pieces; at others he sat at the pianoforte or assumed the principal direction; and not infrequently took all the labor of instructing the solo singers. Though now in his seventieth year, and feeling the approaching failure of his physical powers, the hope became strong that he might live to take part in the celebration of the fiftieth anniversary of the institution. For that occasion he undertook to make such a revision of his old master's *Betulia liberata* as to make it correspond to the demands of the then-present condition of the musical art. His work, however, was interrupted, especially in the autumn of that year (1820) by failing strength and violent pains, which often prevented him from closing his eyes all the night long and, of course, rendered him too weak for any labor for the next following days.

During one of these sleepless nights, he set the following words to music: "Spiritus meus attenuabitur; Dies mei breviabuntur, et solum mihi superest sepulcrum" (My spirit grows feeble; my days are shortened, and to me the tomb alone remains)—a composition which he often sang with his pupils. In the winter his health improved, and his hilarity and pleasure in labor enabled him to bear with the minor ills that still plagued him. In April 1821, he suffered much with his eyes; but the evil being happily overcome, he finished *La Betulia*, shortening the antiquated recitatives and arias, adding choruses and the like; working always in the spirit and style of Gassmann, so effectually as not to disturb the unity of the work. To give a more festive character to the occasion, he composed a march and grand chorus, text by Friedrich Treitschke, to the memory of Gassmann. The chorus was divided into two parts, the first preceded by the march opening the concert, the second being sung after *Betulia*. The first part was sung by a chorus of fifty boys, assembled around a laurel-crowned bust of Gassmann; the second by all the voices present. The concert took place on April 15, under the direction of [Michael] Umlauf, Salieri's eyes preventing him from taking any active part. All the expenses of copying, of the bust, etc. were borne by Salieri and amounted to at least a thousand florins. The concert closed with Klopstock's ode *Frühlingsfeier* (Celebration of Spring) set by Abbé Maximilian Stadler. The next evening the second concert took place at which Haydn's *Creation* was given, his bust standing in front, the cost of which also was borne by Salieri—in short, the entire cost of both concerts was assumed by the now aged composer. Mosel transcribes these words from Salieri's notes upon this occasion: "Thus, I think that I have publicly proved my gratitude to my teacher, father and benefactor, Florian Gassmann, and my veneration for his memory; and that I have thus not unworthily brought my musical life to its close."

His eyes still troubled him and grew dim; yet he could read and write in moderation and take his walks. The next spring (1822) the sleepless nights came again; but, on the whole, he was not dissatisfied for he writes: "I can eat, sing, take walks and gossip; still, however, I think often upon death, and keep myself ready at any moment to receive him."

On the eighth of June, as Anselm Hüttenbrenner says, in the article previously quoted:

Salieri drove with me and another pupil by way of Hütteldorf to Weidlingen[4] [two lovely villages among the hills a few miles west of Vienna], where we wandered long in the romantic garden of Prince Dietrichstein. When we had reached the highest point of the park we sang a trio in praise of the grandeur of creation. The good master was deeply affected and, turning his eyes to the clouds about the setting sun, he said: "I feel that the end of my days is drawing near; my senses are failing me; my delight and strength in creating songs are gone; he, who once was honored by half of Europe, is forgotten; others have come and are the objects of admiration; one must give place to another. Nothing remains for me but trust in God, and the hope of an unclouded existence in the Land of Peace."

This summer, besides keeping up gratis the instruction of his pupils, Salieri amused himself with reading through all his long series of compositions in regular order. As he wrote at that time:

It is a pleasure for me to find more good than bad in them and when, as now and then happens, I am able to improve a passage which had always displeased me but which I was unable to correct, then no one is happier than I. It may be said that a very little, then, can make

[4] Hüttenbrenner's original (see Appendix F for full translation) correctly calls the latter village Weidlingau.—T.A.

me happy; nay, for this only proves the passion of an artist for his art, without which no one would ever produce anything really good.

The January of 1823 was very cold and dry and seemed to give the old man new strength, for his walks were frequently continued three hours without exhausting him, and that too when the snow forced him to confine himself within the city walls. His wet weather work was still instruction, both in the morning hours and after dinner until 5 p.m., while in the evening until ten or eleven o'clock, he was as busy as ever in studying his old compositions, or in writing out those short pieces which he so much delighted to compose.

But the spring was wretchedly cold and rainy, and his health failed rapidly. The sulphur baths at Baden (near Vienna) in the summer, and then the artificial ones at home, helped him somewhat. In October 1823, however, his nervous system broke down, and the last hardly legible words written with his lamed hand are given by Mosel: "Gen. 1824. Dio Santissimo! misericordia di me." (Jan. 1824. Most Holy God! Have mercy upon me.).

There was now no hope that he could ever again officiate in the chapel and he sent in a petition to be pensioned. Count Moritz Dietrichstein (at this present writing, September 1864, confined to his room by extreme old age) had succeeded Kueffstein as *Musikgraf*. He himself was a composer, and for two generations has been one of the musical authorities of Vienna. He was the one to communicate the answer to Salieri's petition, which he did under date June 15, 1824—the 58th anniversary off the petitioner's arrival in Vienna with Gassmann. He wrote:

His Majesty, by decision dated Prague, the 6th of this month, has been pleased to grant the petition, offered of your own free will, to be relieved of further duties, and that, too, with retention of your full salary.

You will have no doubt, I flatter myself, as to the feelings with which I make known this decision—a duty devolving upon me through my official position.

They are the feelings of respect, admiration and gratitude, to which few men in the walks of art have so clear a claim as you.

In the service of four monarchs of the imperial house you have proved an incorruptible truth and devotion, and a perfect self-negation, which have never for a moment wavered, even in the most diverse and, for less magnanimous persons than you, tempting relations.

You have produced a long list of immortal works in almost all branches of music; and, while striving to emulate your great model, Gluck, and your ever honored teacher, Gassmann, you have solidly founded your own fame.

Through your philanthropy, through your peculiar gift for teaching and friendly communication of knowledge, and through the charms of your social qualities, you have made yourself the center of a circle of disciples in art, who must thank you, some for their pecuniary welfare, others for the elevation of their tastes and the purest enjoyment. Your beneficial influence upon the musical art and all others related to it is not to be mistaken; and if the former has wandered into many a by-path, still she will by degrees, like so many other things in this world, find her way back to the true standpoint, and throw new glory around her favorites.

As to myself, through the grace of his Majesty, the Emperor, it has now for six years been my good fortune to be in closer relations to you. I found you already, after fifty years of honorable service, adorned with the marks of imperial favor, with which those of a foreign monarch were joined. I found you in the possession of the respect and affection of your fellow citizens, and of all who favor the loveliest of the arts. And now physical afflictions hindered active duties, and this was sufficient to induce you—you to whom zeal in your office was ever above all else—to that step, which gives you your well-earned repose.

May you enjoy it in full measure; arm yourself, as hitherto, with that greatness of soul, which belongs to a spirit like yours; forget not your noble, irreproachable life, your numberless friends and admirers, and make a place among them for him, who with heartfelt emotion and the expression of his most distinguished respect, now takes leave of you.

Moritz, Count v. Dietrichstein,
Court Musikgraf.

Upon the acceptance of Salieri's resignation, Joseph Eybler, the Vice-Kapellmeister, was advanced to the head of the music in the palace chapel.

It is both amusing and melancholy to read in the Beethoven conversation books, the gossip retailed by his nephew and other intimates. Salieri, as the most distinguished and venerable relic of the preceding generation of Viennese musicians, has his place in that gossip. At one time [ca. December 22-23, 1823], Karl [actually Anton Schindler—T.A.] relates that the poor old broken down man has become so penurious as not to allow his daughters to marry, being unwilling to grant them a dowry! And when the story gains currency that the old composer has confessed his having poisoned Mozart—a story which it is now perfectly well known had no foundation, other than the possible vagaries of insanity—the youth very wisely informs his uncle, that very probably there is something to it!

♯ ♯ ♯ ♯ ♯

{Salieri's mental and physical decline, and Vienna's reaction to it, may be witnessed by a brief chronological survey of entries in Beethoven's conversation books:

Anton Schindler (ca. November 15-21, 1823): They say that Salieri's position will no longer be filled, and that Joseph Eybler alone shall reign.

Nephew Karl (ca. November 23-26, 1823): Salieri has cut his throat, but he is still alive.

Anton Schindler (ca. December 22-23, 1823): Salieri had to be taken to the hospital by force, because he did not want to bear the cost himself. Then, on the second day, while the guards ate lunch, he began to slash away with a table knife, but was restrained from it.... At home he would absolutely take no medicine, and had to be brought.

Nephew Karl (ca. January 21-25, 1824): Salieri declares that he has poisoned Mozart.

Anton Schindler (ca. January 21-25, 1824): With Salieri it is going very badly again. He constantly fantasizes that he is guilty of Mozart's death, and that he gave him poison ... he wants to confess this as such [i.e., to a priest].

Anton Schindler (ca. February 8, 1824): The belief in Salieri's confession is also to be judged in that light [unclear reference in context] ... It is absolutely no proof, it only strengthens the belief.

Johann Schickh, newspaper editor (ca. February 8, 1824): There is a 100 to 1 chance that the utterance of Salieri's conscience is true! ... The method of Mozart's death bears out these remarks.

Anton Schindler (ca. February 8, 1824): You are so gloomy again, sublime Master ... Do not take it so much to heart; it is largely the destiny of great men! ... There are certainly many living who can testify how [Mozart] died, if the *symptoms* appeared ... He [Salieri?] will, however, have harmed Mozart more by his disapproval, than Mozart him.[5]

It becomes apparent that contemplating his former teacher's dissolution and the rumors it produced caused Beethoven considerable anguish, as it must have for many who had known and admired Salieri in his prime.—T.A.}

♯ ♯ ♯ ♯ ♯

The fact is, that after January 1824, Salieri broke down very rapidly, and the entire prostration of his nervous system brought with it mental aberration. But both his physician and his two constant attendants publicly testified—as may be seen in the *Harmonicon IV*, No. 46 (October 1826), p. 190—that no expressions ever passed the sick man's lips in their hearing, which could give color to the idea [that he had poisoned Mozart]. (For the text of their "attestation," see Appendix A.—T.A.)

The old man lingered on through another year, and finally closed his long and useful career at 8 p.m. on May 7, 1825—in the ninth month of his 75th year—and was honored at his funeral [on May 10] by the presence of all the members of the court musical establishment, with Count Dietrichstein at the head, and by all the distinguished composers and musicians then in Vienna.[6]

---

[5] Ludwig van Beethoven, *Konversationshefte*, edited by Karl-Heinz Köhler et al., 12 vols. projected (Leipzig: VEB Deutscher Verlag für Musik, 1968-   ); IV, 252, 259; V, 40-137 passim.

[6] Beethoven's presence is highly unlikely: in poor health himself, he had moved to Baden during the day of May 7, thus a few hours before Salieri died. Since he complained of intestinal inflammation and claimed that he was so weak he could hardly walk properly, it is probable that Beethoven remained in the country on May 10, rather than venture back into the city. Thayer's phrase, translated directly from Mosel, may in fact be a veiled reference to Beethoven's absence.—T.A.

Among his manuscripts was found the *Requiem* already mentioned, entitled by his own hand: "Messa funebre piccola, da me, piccolissimo, Antonio Salieri," which was sung in the Italian church by his pupils, old and new, at the solemn mass to his memory a few days after his burial. Mosel, himself a composer, who knew Salieri intimately, and to whom the papers of the

Antonio Salieri, ca. 1818-19; engraving by Adam Ehrenreich, after a painting by Natale Schiavoni. Detail of painting, reproduced in color, may be found in Alverà, *Rossini,* p. 39.

deceased were entrusted, describes him thus:

Salieri was in stature small rather than large, neither fat nor lean, of a brunette complexion, lively eyes, black hair, temperament choleric, quick-tempered, but able to say with Horace, "tamen ut placabilis essem," for reflection always very quickly took the place of his anger. He was fond of order and neatness; dressed fashionably but always in clothes suited to his years. All games were alike indifferent to him. He drank nothing but water, but was inordinately fond of cake and sweetmeats. Reading, music, and solitary walks were his favorite amusements. Ingratitude was hateful to him; on the contrary, among the pleasantest of his duties were those which a sense of obligation imposed upon him. He enjoyed doing good when he had the opportunity, and his purse was always open to those in need. He liked to talk, especially about his art, a topic on which he was inexhaustible. Sloth was disgusting, skepticism horrible to him. When he was in the wrong he gladly confessed it; and even when in the right, if the dispute was not one touching his honor, or even that of a third person, he not infrequently, for the sake of peace, bore the appearance of being in the wrong. He had a terror of pain and misfortune; when they came, however, he found a support in religion, and patiently bore his afflictions. Discreet praise gave him pleasure; when exaggerated it was painful. At times he was oppressed with a melancholy which he could not explain, and would weep without being able to assign any reason for it. When in these moods he thought often of death, though without fear, and could pass no picturesque group of trees upon an elevated spot without wishing to be buried beneath them. Usually, however, he was in good spirits and full of life; his politeness, his joyous disposition, his jovial and always harmless wit made him one of the pleasantest of companions; this last quality not seldom relieved him when in a strait. On one occasion, a woman who occupied lodgings in a house belonging to Mme. Salieri and her two brothers, demanded some impossible change in the dwelling. She had applied in vain to the elder brother who had charge of the house, and now besieged Salieri who vainly explained to her that this was a matter entirely out of his sphere, that he could not give power to make a change which his brother-in-law had declared impossible, etc. She came again and again, until the composer, having exhausted his explanations, finally closed the business by saying: "Well, madame, so that you may see it is no lack of good will on my part to do what I can for you, just write out your demand and I will set it to music." The woman laughed and left him in peace.

Salieri had made a vow to bestow gratis, that which he received gratis from his benefactor Gassmann. Therefore, he not only instructed young talent, which was to make music the means of subsistence, for nothing, but his receipts for lessons taught to the nobility and the rich were a fund which he distributed among the poor musicians of Vienna.

APPENDICES

Introduction

As a "coda" to his serialization of Salieri's biography, Thayer wrote the following:

"In the Leipzig *Allgemeine musikalische Zeitung*, XII, col. 196, is a communication from Salieri in relation to Gluck's last works, worthy of being translated; in XIII, col. 207, a copy of an order to the imperial orchestra in relation to the proper style of violin playing, equally well worth translation; and in the XXVIIth and XXXth volumes are very interesting reminiscences of him by Rochlitz and Anselm Hüttenbrenner."

Doubtless Thayer would have wanted these included in a full version of his work, and thus they appear here as Appendices B, C, D, E and F. My translations may differ from excerpts included by Thayer in the body of his biography, although not substantially so. In addition, Appendix A contains the "attestation" by Salieri's two attendants during 1824-25; working on the premise that Thayer would have quoted them in full if Dwight had allowed him, I have done so here.

T.A.

APPENDIX A

Attestation of Salieri's Two Attendants, 1825

W E, THE UNDERSIGNED, who are, by profession, attendants on the sick (*infermieri*), declare, in the presence of God and man, that in the spring of 1824, we were called to attend the Cavaliere Salieri, *maestro di capella* to the Royal court, and that during the whole course of his long illness we never quitted him a single moment; that is, when one of us was absent, the other always remained in attendance. We also attest, that in consequence of his weak state, no one was permitted to visit him except ourselves and his medical attendants; it being judged proper that not even the members of his own family should see him. With respect, therefore, to the following question put to us: *Whether it is true that the aforesaid Cavaliere Salieri had said, during his illness, that he had poisoned the celebrated composer Wolfgang Mozart?* —we reply, upon our honor and conscience, that we never heard such words uttered by the said Salieri, nor the slightest mention of anything alluding to it.

In confirmation of this, we subscribe our names as follow:

Giorgio Rosenberg,   Amadeo Porsche,
Infermiere.   *Infermiere presso il Signor Salieri,*
     Maestro di Capella di Corte.

Vienna, June 5, 1825.

N.B. Dr. Rörhik, the medical attendant of Salieri, confirms, as far as his knowledge goes, the above statement made by the two assistant infermieri.

"Mozart and Salieri," *Harmonicon* 4, No. 46 (October 1826), 189-190; the article also includes a letter from Baron Guldner, Vienna, quoting Dr. Closset, Mozart's physician, who stated that the composer had died of an inflammatory fever prevalent in Vienna during Autumn 1791.

APPENDIX B

Salieri on Gluck, 1809

A Declaration by the *Austrian Imperial First Kapellmeister, Antonio Salieri, Vienna, Concerning Rochlitz's Essay, "Gluck's Last Plans and Works," AMZ 11, No. 25 (March 22, 1809), cols. 385-390.*

♯ ♯ ♯ ♯ ♯

It gave me great joy to see the keen interest with which the great Gluck became the subject of conversation—an occasion to which no friend of art can be indifferent—and if I might report something further here, I hope that the wishes of the author [Rochlitz] and all admirers of Gluck might be satisfied! This account is not about me, but rather only the subject himself, about whom a few things can now be clarified.

From my earliest youth on I was a passionate admirer of that great genius and his magnificent works. Through favorable circumstances I not only made his acquaintance, but also, since 1766 (my sixteenth year of life), was taken into his confidence and his home, and remained thus until his death in November 1787. For several years he placed me in charge of his works which were given in Vienna (*Orfeo, Alceste, Paride ed Elena, Iphigenia in Tauris*). Finally, he himself chose me to compose the French opera *Les Danaïdes*, which had been commissioned from him, and in this labor, my first for Paris, I was supported by his invaluable advice. Thus I can confirm, and do confirm herewith, what the author [Rochlitz] asserted about the *Stabat mater*, the *Hermanns-Schlacht* (text: Klopstock), and the Gellert and Klopstock songs.

Specifically, Gluck set nothing in the church style (at least I never heard him mention anything) except a *De profundis*—a piece

which he gave me shortly before his death, to be deposited in the
Collection for Chamber [i.e., household] Music of the Emperor
Joseph II. Joseph wished to hear it, and I had it performed in con-
junction with the funeral Mass held for the departed composer.

Antonio Salieri, in old age. The chain and medal indicate a date after June 1816; the
expression of the face may indicate a period after February 1821 (see Rehberg's engraving, p. xv, above). The original of this widely-reproduced painting is in the Gesellschaft
der Musikfreunde, Vienna; its fullest color likeness in Schmidt-Görg and Schmidt,
Beethoven, p. 233.

The *De profundis*—I must confess—is not written in an overtly *masterly* style (maestralmente) if one specifically means by this expression works full of artifice (in which Gluck placed very little stock); rather, it is indeed written in a truly *Christian* style (cristianamente), and therefore, in my opinion, has far more value for its purpose than so many other works written in the masterly but not a Christian style; these appear to me to be unsuitable and even detrimental for religious use.

Of Gluck's music to the Gellert and Klopstock poems, there exists—for our purposes here—nothing except two small odes which, with very simple piano accompaniment, have been printed in Vienna. The music which the great master created to set the *Hermanns-Schlacht* also does not exist, since he carried it only in his head, but never wrote it down. Several times during the last days of his life, he wanted to dictate a trial version of it to me, since he had lost the use of his right hand through a stroke of apoplexy. Indeed I had heard him sing this piece on various occasions at Court, where, however, he had only the magnificent verbal text in front of him. This little project would probably have been accomplished, too, if Madame Gluck—out of fear that a new stroke of illness might be caused by having his fantasies fired up—had not always asked me to perform some necessary chore or another, which I could not refuse. When Gluck himself finally insisted on this project, the doctor stepped in and, for the same reason, very definitely forbade it. Thus it was, then, that the great mind took these heavenly ideas with him to Heaven. To retain something like this in memory when one has heard it performed, and then to write it down, was therefore not possible because Gluck never sang it the same way twice, and the third time was different still. Each time he modified entire passages to a greater or lesser extent—from which it became evident that he was not entirely in agreement with himself on the matter.

This is all I know to say about this topic and, if not satisfactory, it is nonetheless reliable. I generally doubt that anything more about Gluck's life, educational background and works will be discovered, and most of what we know has been learned from his own reports.

German version, translated from Salieri's Italian, in *Allgemeine musikalische Zeitung* 12 (December 1809), cols. 196-198.

APPENDIX C

Salieri on String Playing, 1811

W E GIVE THE FOLLOWING, *very interesting letter from Antonio Salieri, First Kapellmeister of the Viennese Court, in its entirety, without abbreviation, and in a completely faithful translation of the well-written original Italian. Since its contents and intentions are not without importance, every musician should take its message to heart.—Ed.*

♯ ♯ ♯ ♯ ♯

Since your journal has as its purpose the appreciation and promotion of music, I flatter myself that the communication of this decree by the Direction of the Imperial Theater in Vienna will not displease you. Its contents are as follows:

For some time there has been creeping in among various weak violin soloists a feminine and ridiculous style of handling their instrument, which the Italians call the *maniera smorfiosa* [mincing, affected manner], and consists of a misuse of the travel up and down the strings by the fingers [sliding].

This soft and childish manner has spread like an infectious disease among several orchestra players and, even more ridiculous, not only to the rest of the good violinists, but to violists and even contrabassists as well. When it takes place in the full orchestra, such a practice—because an indulged evil is always aggravated —transforms it from a harmonious body to a gathering of whimpering children or meowing cats.

This method of playing runs contrary to the consideration which every player must apply to strange [i.e., new] compositions, and contrary to the respect which is due the public, which, for its money wants to have music performed seriously and not in a joking manner. Therefore: every director of the Imperial Theater Orchestra in Vienna is hereby notified that he does not have to endure such a tasteless innovation on the part of individuals under his direction. At the same time, every musician, since his honor and salary are dear to him, is likewise notified that if he has those significant mistakes pointed out to him and takes no notice of this direction, he will be declared a poor player, and therefore will be regarded as incapable of remaining any longer in the company of worthy practitioners of his art. This will make it the duty of the Direction to dismiss such a musician.

Note: This ridiculous mannerism on the violin is attributed to a joke by the famous violin player *Lolli.*[1] Since, in his later years, he was no longer the master of the ravishing, magical energy with which he had formerly held the public captive, he sought, in order to win words of praise for the concerts he gave on his tours, at least to give the public something to laugh at—in which he imitated, in the final allegros of his concertos, first the parrot, then the dog, then the cat. The "Cat Concerto," as he himself called it, was *most beloved* by the public, and he therefore gave it most frequently and to universal applause. Not only other violinists, but even violoncellists now sought to imitate this master in his jokes. By and by, the joke became fashion—a fashion which, in its odd way, ravished not only players but also singers of both genders, and ultimately became the method among the weak and the stupid. Since the number of the latter is infinite, the false manner gradually passed into a kind of *school,* from which a fine litter of cats has resulted, who, by their playing and singing in this manner, torment the ears of their listeners with the intention of delighting them. It is to be hoped, however, that this fashion will soon reach its

[1] Antonio Lolli, ca. 1725-1802, specialized in finger glissandi, up and down, through two octaves.—T.A.

end, because the educated public already begins to deride this veritable cat's meowing ... or at least begins to give signs of its displeasure. From now on, it is forbidden to employ players or singers who adhere to this method in either the Court Theaters or in the Musical Society of the city of Vienna.

In making the essence of the above decree known to you, I am convinced that I am performing an agreeable service to composers of all styles. I remain, with greatest esteem, etc.

Allgemeine musikalische Zeitung 13 (March 1811), cols. 207-209.

APPENDIX D

Rochlitz's Meetings with Salieri, 1822

ON THE FIRST DAY OF Pentecost [Whitsunday, May 26, 1822], I attended the morning service at the Imperial *Hofkapelle* (Court Chapel). It is small, about as wide as our St. Peter's Church in Leipzig, and yet somewhat shorter. Everything is very simple, but dignified. In this space and under these conditions is performed, for instance, the music for high mass. None of the blaring, roaring instruments! The proportions are four persons per violin [string?] part and the same number for each vocal part. Other than the quartet [of string parts], it has ony the most absolutely necessary wind instruments. What was formerly played by a large wind section is now entrusted to the organ, which is not strong but has a pretty tone. As I hardly need mention, everything is performed in an exemplary fashion.

The composition I heard was completely suited to all of this: only noble, pious thoughts, neither brilliant nor flashy; a pure, most highly selective style, and yet absolutely uncomplicated artistically; and a faithful, tender expression of the words of the text—no more and no less. It was proper not unto itself, but only as an integral part of the celebration of the religious observance. And thus I only heard the music, I only felt it, until the Offertory which, as you know, marks a division—a certain transitional and resting point—in each service. Here the composer had, with great ardor, set the words of the psalm, *Populi, timete magnum nomen Domini et submissi orate,* and, the greatest simplicity of the style and those very limited performing resources notwithstanding, he truly made the heart tremble and bow down in humble

166

devotion to God. Thus this piece seized me, and thus was my attention especially turned to these expressive tones. After the end of the service, as I was walking in the courtyard of the palace, Kapellmeister [Franz Xaver] Gebauer met me and accompanied me. He asked about that which was most important to him, the music I had just heard, and so I told him approximately what I have just told you.

Two days later [Tuesday, May 28], in the morning, there entered into my lodging a friendly old man, rather small and lean of person, distinguished, with pleasant contours in his face, lively, bright eyes, adroit and fine manners. Appearing to me somewhat over sixty years old (although I learned later that he was ten years older), he came in unannounced because the servant had just been sent out. In a very odd German that I cannot reproduce, he began casually: "Kapellmeister Gebauer told me that you are here in town, and that you were present in His Majesty's Chapel on Pentecost, and that the music of the Offertory pleased you. Allow me, if I might ..." Thereupon he handed me a beautifully written rolled-up score, where my first glance found on the title page, in the Italian language: "In Remembrance of Pentecost in Vienna, 1822—from me, Antonio Salieri." "And you, sir," I said, "are ...?" "I'm old Salieri." You can imagine what joy that gave me!

We had hardly sat down when we were deep in conversation, as if I had known him for years. By occasioning the gift, which I still held in my hand, I had, without knowing it, awakened in him a favorite topic of conversation: the exact knowledge, distinction, separation and strong opinions about the various genres of music, and the style appropriate to each in the artistic period now coming to an end, in contrast to the style presently on the rise, with its mixture of everything. "Leading to the development of a new style, which then, on a higher plane, hopefully might be separated again ...," I inserted. "If the Lord God grants it," he said pensively. Then, to be sure, he added more about the earlier conditions in music, and their strict conformity to theoretical principles which he considered as respectable and laudable for so many years, and therefore still did now. As openly as he confessed this, he still expressed himself against the opposing view with intellect and feeling, and in no way with hostility. He spoke on the subject in a sagacious, appropriate, concise and very lively manner; his tone of voice was ringing, firm and clear, like an Italian tenor; his eyes sparkled, and it was so engaging that his mein and mood always remained serene, even cheerful. And what language this was! When German escaped him in the heart of conversation, it was replaced by Italian, mixed with French; whereupon he smilingly excused himself: "I have only been in Germany for over fifty years! How could I have learned the language yet?" You cannot believe how amiable was this old man, who, very deservingly, is famed far and wide.

After this we came, by way of example, to Haydn and Mozart. He spoke of their works with the benevolent appreciation of an old man and the cheerful love of a youth. He declared his favorites among Haydn's works to be the string quartets and *Die Schöpfung.* "And the symphonies?" I asked. "Oh!" he cried, and kissed the tips of his fingers, "but with a few of the last ones excepted, they do not adhere to the style consistently, and now and again encroach upon the string quartet."

Among Mozart's works he especially loved the quartets as well, and of all the operas, *Figaro.* "But the concertos ...?" He confessed to me that, in the realm of precious thoughts completely in his style, as well as in artful and heartfelt execution, they were perhaps to be placed at the head of all of Mozart's instrumental pieces. But, he explained, they also (and especially the last ones) exceed the style in exquisite development, and yet, given the tonally-poor pianoforte, they do not serve well as concertos for today's virtuosos. "And the *Requiem* ...?" Ah, he said with solemnity, that exceeds all norms! Here is where Mozart, after a very dissipated life, and faced with his own death, was seized by a spirit of Eternity, a Holy Spirit. (In all of this I am not giving you his exact words, but rather their meaning.)

Then we came to his great teacher (after Gassmann's death)— to Gluck. His heart burst forth in veneration, love and gratitude. Here I sought to keep him on the subject, for how much is written about Gluck, and how easily comprehensible does the essence of his later works of art, from *Iphigenia in Aulis* on, seem to us—and yet we still do not possess a complete, coherent, fully rounded, satisfactory portrait of him, either as a great man or as a human being; it is only a concept, not a reality.

Salieri gave me such a portrait (Who could do something like this off the top of his head?); he told me many interesting things which could be used: about Gluck's life, about the manifold worldly and social influences on his soul, about his method of study—to prepare himself, and then to compose—etc. I cannot repeat it here, however; it ranges too far and wide. Our visit together lasted almost two hours.

Afterwards I saw the worthy man several more times. He brought me still another beautiful setting of a psalm which he had composed, and wrote a kind dedication on the title page. I will recall here only his last visit, the day before my departure. At that time he told me many things about the course of his private and public life from early on, about his manner of working and also about his religious views. And, as he took his farewell, he said, not without solemnity, that whether I remembered it or not, we would see each other again in four weeks! Then he explained that a seventy-year-old man must take every farewell as if it were forever. And then I had to give him my word that if God called him, I would report something of what he had told me (and which might be remotely sympathetic to him) in the *Musikalische Zeitung*. If I survive him, I shall certainly keep my word. [Postscript, 1828: I have kept it as well as possible, given these fragmentary accounts. Otherwise the reader knows that later, in 1827, Herr von Mosel in Vienna produced a complete biography of Salieri, partially from the papers left in his estate.]

For you, dear Härtel, I will only add the following: Thus, Salieri is a kind, cheerfully comprehensible, highly agreeable man; and I tell you this, even though he is not someone [whose works] you desire [to publish], so that you will not misunderstand him or do him injustice. He absolutely does not want to publish anything more. "Since I retired from the opera," he said, "I have written nothing except little social songs, canons and such, especially those to be sung outdoors [and the poetry for them was partly by him] and church music. The world possesses what I have written for it; those little pieces are for my friends; these sacred works are for God and my Emperor." That is something which one must acknowledge with honor, I think, and not seek to destroy.

Friedrich Rochlitz to Gottfried Christoph Härtel, Baden, July 9, 1822; published in *Allgemeine musikalische Zeitung* 30 (January 1828), cols. 7-10. The total letter/article is considerably longer and also deals with Rochlitz's visits with Beethoven, the last of which must have occurred in September 1822.

Rochlitz upon Salieri's Death, 1825

Antonio Salieri

IMPERIAL AUSTRIAN FIRST Kapellmeister, Member of the Academies of Art in Paris, Stockholm, etc.

NECROLOGY

The rough storms which now lead us into Spring have extinguished the now-exhausted little flame of life from one of our most ingenious, most knowledgeable, and most famous musicians—named above. If Salieri's death now creates no sensation, perhaps painfully perceived only by those who were personally close to him, still it reflects in no way upon his merits and virtues—as if they were suitable only for the moment, with that moment passed; nor does it reflect any injustice by his contemporaries—as if they had not acknowledged those merits or forgotten them. Rather, it reflects upon the circumstances deriving partly from the length of his life and from the images [of old age and illness] which come to virtually each person; and partly from the lack of perception of his later activity withdrawn from the world at large.

For a long time he made no particular effort to further his great reputation, and a reputation—like any good fortune —which is not furthered, is diminished. Thus it transpired that for the past two years (at least as concerns his activities, to which he remained dedicated until that time) he already seemed completely sunken into death.

If we call him one of our own, it is not reckoned upon his origins and earliest youth, but rather his almost sixty-year residence in Germany and (more decisively for him as an artist) the spirit, the taste, and also the manner in which he wrote the best of his many works. With few unimportant exceptions, as concerns the opera, these were not even written to German texts, but rather Italian or French. Still, in spirit, taste and method of handling, these were really German [*sic!*]. In a manner peculiarly his own, he was able to combine the grace, intelligibility, and elegance of the [style] period before last: indeed it gave his operas a peculiar charm and individuality which no others possessed. As for his church compositions, they are so completely and purely German that no such qualifications of opinion need be added. (Only in his youth did he write a few pleasant little pieces for instruments.)

# # # # #

Antonio Salieri was born in 1750, of a wealthy and respected family in the Venetian territories, and from early childhood enjoyed the best possible upbringing in terms of education and life in general. In the course of his training, since he had demonstrated a talent and inclination for music early on, he took up this art as a part of his overall studies, and as a means of giving pleasure to himself and those around him. But his father was a merchant engaged in a large, dangerous overseas trade. When this failed, he lost by far the greatest portion of his fortune, while dishonesty on the part of several other businessmen nearly finished him off. Worry over these circumstances and the strangeness of the new lifestyle they made necessary rushed him to his grave, and the many children he left behind were thus forced to make their own fortunes.

Antonio already played the cembalo well and sang excellent soprano. He was accepted into one of Venice's foremost monastery schools, where (since he entered as first soprano in the church choir) he received room, board, and an education, as well as further instruction in music. He now resolved to dedicate his whole life to this art; and since his talent for it was by now unmistakable, and since his love, zeal, and diligence burned for it, no one objected to his doing so.

Now Kapellmeister Gassmann enters the picture—an excellent

man, both as a human being and as a composer, whose fame is
not generally known today because he wrote almost exclusively
for the church [*sic*] and died young. The Viennese Court sent
him to Italy to recruit singers for the recently established Opera.
Gassmann heard Antonio sing in church, was joyously surprised,
inquired about him and, after a full tour of Italy, took him to
Vienna where he introduced the youth to Emperor Joseph. The
monarch was pleased not only with the singing, but also with the
moral and modest, as well as the simultaneously cheerful and
ingenuous nature of this amiable young man, and turned him
over to Gassmann, to care for in his house and to further his
higher education in music. Antonio sang in the *Hofkapelle* [Court
Chapel] and was entirely fortunate in his favor with the Emperor,
in the love of his teacher, in his art, and in his now worry-free
youth.

But he had come to Vienna in his sixteenth year of life, and it
was not long before his attractive soprano voice began to waver,
and then to break. This and the most vigorous inclination
(which developed from the fullness of his talents) induced Antonio to devote himself to composition, under Gassmann's guidance. The teacher set rigid standards—according to the earlier,
well-grounded practice—first in church composition, and only in
later years in operatic writing, without, however, permitting
Salieri—and with good reason—to present his youthful creations
in public. Now Gassmann died, and the Ritter Gluck who,
crowned with glory, had returned from France and was living a
quiet life, did for Antonio what earlier had been done for himself. Several of his works were made known to the Emperor
Joseph, who in ca. 1775, appointed Salieri as his Kapellmeister.

Enriched by Gluck's ever more successful operas, the Paris
Theater Administration pressed him to write a new work in this
style, and sent him the libretto for *Les Danaïdes*. Judicious and
discreet as he was, Gluck, now in his old age, did not want to
jeopardize his reputation before the fickle public, and instead
had Salieri, under his watchful eye and counsel, compose the
opera. He sent the younger man with the completed work to
Paris, without declaring, at least publicly, anything further about
the opera. The Administration saw it to their advantage to let the
public believe that the music was by Gluck. The opera was an

outstanding success (it was again in Paris only a few years ago!), and now Gluck declared publicly that it was by Salieri; whereupon the Parisian critics found that they had noticed something unusual right away, for the style was not completely like Gluck's, but was much more mixed with Italian vocal style and workmanship. In the latter case they were right, for this marks the personalized style which he employed in all his operas. Richly paid, Salieri returned to Vienna. His fame was now secure; everyone wanted operas from him. Through the abundant fountain of invention which flowed from him, and through his great industriousness, he produced a considerable number of works in almost all the genres. Every one found applause, and several of the most outstanding supported him [financially] until his death. The special favor of his Emperor [Joseph II] as well as the present Emperor [Franz I] remained with him. And so his life elapsed, without any remarkable alterations, for almost half a century. Thus we will not dwell upon the minor incidents, but still have to report the following.

With the completion of his fiftieth year of life, Salieri decided to withdraw from composing for the theater, where fresh, youthful fantasy and swift, lively sensation were especially desired, and to dedicate himself to church composition. He was, at the same time, relieved of the administration of the Opera.

In the early years of his adulthood, they say that Salieri not infrequently played serious games with his German rivals for [the Emperor] Joseph's favor and for influence in the theater, and given [Salieri's] Italian nature, with a temperament easily aroused to violence, this [accusation] may not be without grounds. But it is certain that he later spoke out against the advantages given to foreigners, especially those which seemed unjust or which betrayed the laws of Art—and thus he joyfully meted out their full due to Haydn and, later, to Mozart.

One fine, praiseworthy honor accrued from his middle age to his last years: mindful of what had happened to him in his youth, Salieri gave guidance and assistance to talented composers, and a thorough and complete education to youthful singers of both genders, refusing all compensation for it. To the credit of the sublime master, the finest of them often became successful. Joseph Weigl was among the composers. Among the singers, the first were the orphaned daughters of his teacher, Gassmann. The orphaned daughters of the estimable [Anton] Wranitzky, Madame Seidler in Berlin and Madame Kraus in Vienna, were among his last students.

Old age appeared to wait a long time in taking its toll from him. Lively, bright, active, modest, particpating in everything concerning his friends and his art, gentle in his judgments, and simple in the orderliness of his life, conscientious and devout, but without any tendency to bigotry, benevolent more in confidence than paraded before the world, intimate, considerate in social situations, fine and delightful—thus I saw him as late as the summer of 1822 in Vienna, in his 72nd year of life, and spent many pleasant hours with him (and yet not filled with idle chatter), which I shall not forget as long as I live.

Soon afterward, old age suddenly attacked him with all its might, and so heavily that it made its claims all at one time: his hearing grew weak; his thoughts not infrequently became confused; all mental and physical powers declined suddenly; and a complete despondency, alternating with gloomy groundless musings, took possession of him. He had to be relieved of his office as Director of Church Music for the *Hofkapelle*; it was done with the greatest delicacy, also without taking from him the earnings he derived from that office. But the lack of activity only aggravated his troubled condition: his thoughts became confused more often; he lost himself deeper in those black pictures of his waking dreams—deeper until he became completely oblivious, to such an extent that once, while unguarded, he almost wounded himself to death. At other times he accused himself of such crimes as would not have occurred even to his enemies.

Finally, all his friends and the world could only wish for his peaceful passing. Last May 7, this wish was fulfilled.

# # # # #

It is not necessary to say many words about the artistic character of his works and about their artistic value. The most recent ones are still fresh in our memory, as are the opinions of the most estimable experts of all nations where music is cultivated, and all are essentially of a single voice. Among his operas, his ingenious and soulful *Tarare*, written to Beaumarchais' libretto for Paris (or, as it was called after the revision for Emperor Joseph, *Axur, Re d'Ormus*) was accepted with the greatest applause. Even now, in an "old age" which operas seldom attain, *Axur* is still well received in Germany and France. Among his other operas must especially be cited *Les Danaïdes, Il talismano, La grotta di Trofonio, La cifra, Palmira,* and *Cesare in Farmacusa.* All of these have also been produced in translation in German theaters.

His church compositions are not known at all outside of Vienna, since he wrote them all only for his Emperor's Hofkapelle, but they certainly deserve to be known. In spirit and style of writing they may be compared with those of Joseph Haydn, among those of an earlier age. But since the area of the Chapel is small and can accommodate only a few musicians, they are less richly orchestrated. They are also constructed in a less overtly artistic style, especially as regards fugue and counterpoint in general; and yet they have a decidedly lyrical character which gives a fine overall impression. I know several of these pieces, which I must count among the finest of the modern age in their simple nobility, piety, gentleness, and inspiration.

According to public reports, Salieri left handwritten materials concerning the history of his interior and exterior life, and these have been given to one of his trusted friends. If Salieri had had time to write his own life's story, the material (from what we have learned of it) would perhaps have far more interest than one might expect from the biography of a musician. According to his parting words to me when we last saw each other, I shall not wait for that biography, but rather will place my unpretentious sheet of paper upon the pile. The historical material about his earlier life which is given here came from his own mouth. If not a few facts from these and later times are imparted to us by the documents in his *Nachlass* (estate), we will perhaps report them in a later issue.

[Friedrich] Rochlitz

Allgemeine musikalische Zeitung 27 (June 1825), cols. 408-414.

Anselm Hüttenbrenner on Salieri, 1825

A Small Contribution to Salieri's Biography
by Anselm Hüttenbrenner

THROUGH THE RECOMMENDATION of Count Moritz von Fries, an extremely magnanimous promoter of the arts, I was accepted by the I.R. Court Kapellmeister Salieri as a pupil in composition in 1815. The preliminary examination which I underwent beforehand consisted of the following: that I sing a rather difficult *canon a due* with him; then that I play a sonata by Beethoven placed before me; and finally that I must improvise [*praeludieren*]. To the question as to which clefs were most familiar to me, I replied that I was fairly familiar with all of them, whereupon he began to speak of the baritone and half-soprano clefs, and I had to blush in my ignorance of them.

Salieri used no textbook in his instruction in the art of composition. He did not prescribe for his students what they should compose; each had free choice according to his talents and inclinations. In a strict manner the teacher went through whatever was placed before him for correction. He noted fifths and octaves with a mild warning, but an ascending minor seventh was a thorn in the eye to him. The same held true for chord progressions which are difficult for singers to negotiate, and the so-called false relations (*relationes non harmonicae*); he made their ill effects very obvious to us by pounding them sharply on the piano. He was most strict when it came to modulation: he railed vehemently against the constant and glaring changes of key which have become so common in recent times, and compared several modern composers to people who jump out of the window to get to the street. With vocal pieces which were brought to him, he first read over the words with great attention; then he checked the music to see if the character of the poem had been faithfully set. If this were not the case, then the work (even when it contained good and original passages) had absolutely no value in his eyes. On such an occasion, he really flew into a passion and cited many passages from works by famous masters who had made the same type of mistake. In church compositions he would go over the material for the spirit of devotion and prevailing humility: a pompous *Kyrie*, a cheerful *Dona nobis* were odious to him. With operas (he wrote fifty-two of them) he surveyed them to see which character had to sing in this or that musical number. He complained about those composers who had squires sing in the same heroic style as knights, or who had masters trilling as frivolously as their apprentices. He also found it senseless, in less passionate scenes, to employ a great number of instruments, and, without cause, to torment the ear with cruel chords (as he called them), such as might best be suitable for a chorus of Spirits from Hell. According to his view, the opera composer should not be a painter of miniature portraits, and should not engage in tedious repetitions of certain figurations and other contrapuntal affectations. He demanded large, bold strokes to produce the same effect as that of the scene painter.

He considered Gluck to be the greatest opera composer; he alone had portrayed characters most richly in tones, and knew how to bring about the greatest effect with the fewest notes, while in recent times people are no longer deeply moved by even the most monstrous masses of tone, because they are applied all too frequently.

He always spoke of Mozart with exceptional respect. Mozart, the unexcelled one, often came to Salieri with the words, "Dear Papa, give me several old scores from the Court Library; I want to leaf through them with you"—and while doing so, he many times missed his lunch.[1] One day I asked Salieri to show me the house where Mozart died, upon which he led me to the Rauhen-

---

[1] Salieri was actually less than six years older than Mozart. Doubtless either Hüttenbrenner or Salieri (in his own old age) was fantasizing this phraseology.—T.A.

steingasse and did so. If I remember correctly, it is designated by a portrait of [the Virgin] Mary.[2] Salieri visited him on the day before he died, and was one of the few who accompanied his body [at the funeral].

In service to the Court Chapel Salieri was extremely zealous, and in later times even to the detriment of his health. He enjoyed telling jokes, and during excursions out into the country with his students, especially liked to sing canons of a humorous nature; on such occasions he also carried many sugar cookies in his pocket. Transposition gave him particular pleasure, and while in musical circles he was visibly delighted when one of the female singers present placed an aria too high or too low. When a child, he was sentenced to subsist on bread and water because of some merry prank. To everyone's amazement, however, little Toni took his punishment patiently, until it was discovered that he was nourished by sugar which, with forethought, he had hoarded in a hidden place in case he got hungry. He wrote his first opera without his teacher Gassmann's prior knowledge. He often laughed over the fact that, on the day of the first performance, he ran around to all the gates in Vienna looking for his name on every poster.

On June 8, 1822, Salieri drove with me and another student by way of Hütteldorf to Weidlingau, where we wandered for a long time in the romantic garden of Prince Dietrichstein. When we had reached the highest point in the park, we sang a trio in praise of the grandeur of creation. The good master was deeply affected, and turning his eyes to the clouds about the setting sun, he said: "I feel that the end of my days is drawing near; my senses are failing me; my delight and strength in creating songs are gone; he who once was honored by half of Europe is forgotten; others have come and are the objects of admiration; one must give place to another. Nothing remains to me but trust in God, and the hope of an untroubled existence in the Land of Peace."

Jean Paul [1763-1825] was able to describe such holy moments in words which are more moving, and which stir the strings of the soul more powerfully than echoes of the distant harmonies. One passage from his *Blumenstücke* [1796/97] might well be

---

[2] The house and Mozart's apartment are described and illustrated in H.C. Robbins Landon, *1791, Mozart's Last Year* (New York: Schirmer Books, 1988), pp. 201-208.—T.A.

appropriate here. It goes like this:

There are dreadful twilight moments in us, when—as day and night divide; as we might as easily be created or annihilated; as the Theater of Life and its audience respond to one another—our role has passed: we stand alone in the darkness, but we still wear the theatrical costume, and we see ourselves in it and ask ourselves: "What are you now, Self?" When we ask thus, then there is nothing great or secure for us anymore—everything will be an eternal cloud of night, in which there is sometimes a glimmer, but it sinks ever deeper with heavier drops—and only high above the cloud is there a brilliance, and that is God, and far below it is a speck of light, and that is Mankind-Self.

And after that evening, I never saw Maestro Salieri again.

Allgemeine musikalische Zeitung 27 (November 1825), cols. 796-799.

Bibliography

Alverà, Pierluigi. *Rossini,* trans. by Raymond Rosenthal. New York: Treves Publishing Co., 1986.

Anderson, Emily, ed. *The Letters of Mozart and his Family,* third edition. New York: W.W. Norton, 1985.

Angermüller, Rudolph. "Antonio Salieri," *New Grove Dictionary of Music and Musicians,* ed. by Stanley Sadie. 20 vols. London: Macmillan, 1980; vol. 16, pp. 415-420.

Angermüller, Rudolph. *Antonio Salieri: Sein Leben und seine weltlichen Werke.* 3 vols. to date. Munich: Musikverlag Emil Katzbichler, 1971- .

Beethoven, Ludwig van. *Konversationshefte,* ed. by Karl-Heinz Köhler, Gritta Herre et al. 9 vols. to date. Leipzig: VEB Deutscher Verlag für Musik, 1968- .

Einstein, Alfred. *Gluck,* trans. by Eric Blom. London: J.M. Dent and Sons, 1936.

Frimmel, Theodor von. *Beethoven Jahrbuch II.* Munich: Georg Müller, 1909.

Holmes, Edward. *The Life of Mozart, Including his Correspondence.* New York: Harper & Bros., 1845 (repr. 1854, 1860).

Hüttenbrenner, Anselm. "Kleiner Beitrag zu Salieri's Biographie." *Allgemeine musikalische Zeitung* 27 (November 1825), cols. 796-799.

Jahn, Otto. *W.A. Mozart.* 4 vols. Leipzig: Breitkopf und Härtel, 1856-1859.

Landon, H.C. Robbins. *Haydn: Chronicle and Works.* 5 vols. Bloomington: Indiana University Press, 1976-1980.

Landon, H.C. Robbins. *Haydn: A Documentary Study*. New York: Rizzoli, 1981.

Mosel, Ignaz Franz von. *Über das Leben und die Werke des Anton Salieri*. Vienna: J.B. Wallishausser, 1827.

"Mozart and Salieri." *The Harmonicon* 4, No. 46 (October 1826), 189-190.

Ochs, Michael. "A.W. Thayer, the Diarist, and the Late Mr. Brown: A Bibliography of Writings in *Dwight's Journal of Music*." *Beethoven Essays: Studies in Honor of Elliot Forbes*, ed. by Lewis Lockwood and Phyllis Benjamin. Cambridge, Massachusetts: Harvard University Department of Music, 1984; pp. 78-95.

Prieger, Erich. "Alexander Wheelock Thayer." *General-Anzeiger für Bonn und Gegend* (July 27, 1897); trans. by John S. Shedlock, *The Monthly Musical Record 27* (September 1, 1987), 195-196.

Rochlitz, Friedrich. "Antonio Salieri: Nekrolog." *Allgemeine musikalische Zeitung 27* (June 1825), cols. 408-414.

Rochlitz, Friedrich. "Zusatz aus einem spätern Briefe." *Allgemeine musikalische Zeitung 30* (January 1828), cols. 3-16.

Salieri, Antonio. "Erklärung in Beziehung auf Rochlitz's Aufsatz: Glucks letzte Plane und Arbeiten." *Allgemeine musikalische Zeitung* 12 (December 1809), cols. 196-198.

Salieri, Antonio. ["Verordnung des Directoriums der kaiserlichen Theater zu Wien: Brief."] *Allgemeine musikalische Zeitung* 13 (March 1811), cols. 207-209.

Schmidt-Görg, Joseph and Hans Schmidt, eds. *Ludwig van Beethoven*. Bonn: Beethoven-Archiv/Hamburg: Deutsche Grammophon, 1970/1974.

Shaffer, Peter. *Amadeus: A Play*. London: André Deutsch, 1980. Rev. ed. New York: Harper & Row, 1981.

Slonimsky, Nicolas. "The Weather at Mozart's Funeral." *Musical Quarterly* 46 (1960), 12-21.

Thayer, Alexander Wheelock. "Half a Dozen of Beethoven's Contemporaries: II. Antonio Salieri." *Dwight's Journal of Music* 23 (February 20, 1864), 185-187; (March 5, 1864), 193-194; (March 19, 1864), 201-202; 24 (April 2, 1864), 209-210; (April 16, 1864), 217-218; (April 20, 1864), 225-226; (May 14, 1864),

233-234; (May 28, 1864), 241-242; (June 11, 1864), 249-250; (June 25, 1864), 257-258; (July 9, 1864), 265-267; (July 23, 1864), 273-275; (August 6, 1864), 281-282; (August 20, 1864), 289-290; (September 3, 1864), 297-298; (October 15, 1864), 321-322; (October 29, 1864), 329-330; (November 12, 1864), 337-338; (November 26, 1864), 345-347.

Thayer, Alexander Wheelock. "Opera in the Family Hapsburg. Being preliminary to Number Two of 'Half a Dozen of Beethoven's Contemporaries.'" *Dwight's Journal of Music* 23 (December 26, 1863), 153-154; (January 9, 1864), 161-162; (January 23, 1864), 169-170; (February 6, 1864), 177-178.

Wessely, Othmar. "Antonio Salieri." *Die Musik in Geschichte und Gegenwart,* ed. by Friedrich Blume. 17 vols. Kassel: Bärenreiter-Verlag, 1949-86; vol. 11 (1963), cols. 1295-1302.

Index